D0844458

Instructor Competencies

Standards for Face-to-Face, Online, and Blended Settings

Instructor Competencies

Standards for Face-to-Face, Online, and Blended Settings

James D. Klein
Arizona State University

J. Michael Spector
Florida State University

Barbara Grabowski
Pennsylvania State University

Ileana de la Teja
*LICEF Research Center,
Télé-université*

INFORMATION AGE
PUBLISHING

80 Mason Street • Greenwich, Connecticut 06830 • www.infoagepub.com

Library of Congress Cataloging-in-Publication Data

Instructor competencies : standards for face-to-face, online, and
blended settings / James D. Klein ... [et al.].– Rev. 3rd ed.
    p. cm.
 Includes bibliographical references and index.
 ISBN 1-59311-236-X (pbk.) – ISBN 1-59311-237-8 (hardcover)
 1. Employee training personnel. 2. Computer-assisted instruction. 3.
Performance standards. I. Klein, James D.
 HF5549.5.T7I463 2004
 658.3'12404–dc22

                                       2004019604

Published in cooperation with the International Board
of Standards for Training, Performance, and Instruction (ibstpi)
and the Association for Educational Communications and
Technology (AECT).

Copyright Notice

The instructor competencies and performance statements described in this book are
copyrighted by the International Board of Standards for Training, Performance,
and Instruction (ibstpi). All rights reserved.

Copyright © 2004 Information Age Publishing Inc.

All rights reserved. No part of this publication may be reproduced, stored in a
retrieval system, or transmitted, in any form or by any means, electronic, mechanical,
photocopying, microfilming, recording or otherwise, without written permission
from the publisher.

Printed in the United States of America

*This book is dedicated to Rita Richey, former board member
and advisor to the International Board of Standards for Training,
Performance and Instruction. We are indebted to Rita for her inspired
vision of how competencies should be developed and validated.
We admire her persistence for empirical data
and evidence-based decision making.*

THE IBSTPI BOARD

The International Board of Standards for Training, Performance and Instruction (ibstpi) consists of 15 professionals elected to broadly represent academia, businesses, consultancies, and government agencies throughout the world. The board grew out of a certification task force established in 1977 by the Association for Educational Communications and Technology (AECT) and the National Society for Performance and Instruction (now the International Society for Performance Improvement). In 1984, ibstpi became an independent, not-for-profit organization dedicated to increasing the capability of individuals and organizations in the training, instruction, learning, and performance improvement professions through the development of competency-based standards.

When ibstpi approved the instructor competencies described in this book, the Board consisted of the following individuals:

Name	Affiliation	Country
Michiko Achilles	Merrill Lynch	Japan
Ileana de la Teja	LICEF, Télé-université	Canada
Dennis Fields	St. Cloud State University	United States
Marguerite Foxon	Motorola University	United States
Barbara L. Grabowski	Pennsylvania State University	United States
James D. Klein	Arizona State University	United States
John O'Connor	Hutchinson3g	United Kingdom
Roderick Sims	Deakin University	Australia
H. Barbara Sorensen	Air Force Research Laboratory	United States
Timothy W. Spannaus	Wayne State University	United States
J. Michael Spector	Syracuse University	United States
Juan Pablo Ventosa	EPISE Group	Spain
Jan Visser	Learning Development Institute	France/USA

Two previous members were serving as Board Advisors when these competencies were approved and contributed substantially to their development:

- Rita Richey (Wayne State University, United States)
- Robert C. Roberts (Bob Roberts and Associates, United States)

Additionally, other previous ibstpi members made substantial contributions, including:

- Kristian Folkman (Norwegian Trade and Technology Office, Norway)
- Peter Goodyear (Lancaster University, United Kingdom)
- Jelke van der Pal (National Aerospace Laboratory, The Netherlands)
- Mark Teachout (USAA, United States)
- Diane Wagner (consultant, United States)

CONTENTS

FOREWORD

What does it take to be a competent instructor? That simple question is the focus of this entire volume. This volume is, of course, an update of the well-known ibstpi instructor competencies.

This edition is not just a rehash of old, albeit classic and still important, stuff. Instead, it provides a fresh perspective on a topic of perennial interest for those working in the field that has been variously called training and development, human resource development, performance technology, and workplace learning and performance. The fresh perspective takes into consideration two additional instructor settings to the traditional face-to-face environments that most instructors and trainers know—that is, online and blended settings. These settings are, of course, becoming more critical as instruction moves beyond classroom settings to include virtual and combinations of classroom and other media delivery methods.

The ibstpi instructor competencies match up well to *Mapping the Future* (Bernthal et al., 2004), the current ASTD competency study of the field now known as Workplace Learning and Performance (WLP) and previously known as Training and Development (T&D). WLP is more than a new name for an old subject and represents a fundamental paradigm shift in what it means to be a professional in the field formerly known as training. WLP is all about getting improved performance—and therefore improved results—in organizational settings through planned and unplanned learning interventions. Instruction is thus a means to an end and not an end in itself. The ibstpi instructor competencies dovetail well with that philosophy.

Whenever I read a book, I always ask myself three key questions as I go through it: (1) so what? (2) now what? and (3) then what? Addressing these three questions will be the remaining focus of this foreword.

Instructor Competencies: Standards for Face-to-Face, Online, and Blended Settings, pages xiii–xv
Copyright © 2004 by Information Age Publishing
All rights of reproduction in any form reserved.

SO WHAT?

The question "*so what?*" means "*why is this work important?*" It seems that the answer to this question should be self-evident. The work of educators and trainers alike has long focused around conveying information and stimulating people to come up with new ideas. That has never been more important than it is now in an age in which the human capacity to generate new ideas can spell the difference between employment and unemployment for individuals, between competitive success and bankruptcy for businesses, and between success in the global marketplace and failure for nations.

Of course, new technology has added a new spin to the age-old practice of instruction, which some might call the second-oldest profession. With new technology many people are challenged to rethink and even reinvent the traditional role of instructor as purveyor of information in face-to-face settings. Technology may also present a challenge to learners, who must rethink their mental models of what an instructor is supposed to do, how an instructor is supposed to do that, and what role the learner should take in that process. Indeed, in technologically supported instructional formats, learner competence becomes more important (see Rothwell, 2002).

NOW WHAT?

The question "*now what?*" means "*what should you (the reader) do with what you have learned from the book?*" The answer to that question has to do with using the ibstpi competency model. Of course, competency models may be foundational for HR systems for organizations and thereby become the operating system that unifies all HR practices—such as recruiting, selecting, orienting, training, appraising, and rewarding staff (Dubois & Rothwell, 2004). A competency model describes what should be. It is foundational for comparing individuals and groups against a desirable standard.

Competency models may also be a useful reference point for individuals. Indeed, individuals may compare themselves to the model to identify areas for improvement and areas of special strength. The identification of these gaps can then become the focus of improvement efforts.

THEN WHAT?

The question "*then what?*" means "*how could you (the reader) go beyond what you have learned and applied from the book to find creative applications?*" The answer to this question has to do with going beyond what is written in this book to generate new ideas and come up with creative approaches that push what has been learned to new levels. In short, how can the book's contents be pushed to new levels—perhaps well beyond what the authors originally intended?

The authors—James D. Klein, J. Michael Spector, Barbara Grabowski, and Ileana de la Teja—have provided the results of outstanding research on what it takes to be effective as a competent instructor in these (trying) times. My special challenge to you, the reader, is to think beyond what is here to creative ideas, research agendas, and next-steps that push the boundaries further.

—William J. Rothwell
Pennsylvania State University

William J. Rothwell, Ph.D. is Professor of Human Resource Development in the Department of Adult Education, Instructional Systems, and Workforce Education and Development, College of Education on the University Park campus of the Pennsylvania State University. Also the President of Rothwell & Associates, he numbers over 32 multinational corporations on his client list.

PREFACE

For most people, the instructor is the face of training. This role is so emphasized that instructors may be called "trainers" in some environments. In other cultures and environments, instructors may be called teachers, facilitators, tutors, coaches, or many other names. Yet all share the key role of working directly with others to facilitate learning and performance.

In keeping with a 20-year history and mission to develop, validate, and promote the implementation of international standards to advance training, instruction, learning, and performance improvement for individuals and organizations, the International Board of Standards for Training, Performance and Instruction (ibstpi) has documented the changing roles of instructors over the years. In 1988 and 1993, the Board published versions of *Instructor Competencies: The Standards.* Those publications captured the contemporary understanding of an instructor's role—working with students in a face-to-face environment by delivering lectures, giving demonstrations, facilitating discussions, and administering quizzes and other assessments. Instructors in these settings worked with learners who were located in one room at the same time. This model also assumed, explicitly or usually implicitly, that the instructor was the prime actor in the room. Student learning depended in large part on how well the instructor carried out his or her role.

Since 1993, technology and a new emphasis on the active role of learners (which was really always there, but is more prominent now) have changed our perspectives on what good instructors do. Distance learning, e-learning, and other computer-mediated methods have become commonplace, even gracing the covers of business journals and popular magazines, where once they were found only in specialized journals. Of course, many instructors still teach in face-to-face classroom settings. The active learning, learner-centered perspective reminds us that learners in all settings bring knowledge, experi-

Instructor Competencies: Standards for Face-to-Face, Online, and Blended Settings, pages xvii–xviii
Copyright © 2004 by Information Age Publishing
All rights of reproduction in any form reserved.

ence, and perspectives to learning that can benefit everyone in the learning situation and that it is they who bring personal meaning to what they learn.

These two trends change our expectations of instructors. The use of technology to mediate communication between and among instructors, learners, and information requires a new elaboration and interpretation of basic tenets of instruction and learning. Following these paradigms, instructors now serve in multiple roles as conductor, stage crew, coach, and critic as they take, share, or release leadership with and to the learner. Reexamination of these basic tenets does not preclude that some of these approaches would be familiar to correspondence school teachers of many years ago, who also had to depend on technology to mediate communication, even if the technology was ink on paper. Yet the widespread implementation of distance learning requires empirical study of approaches to instruction and learning that go beyond the anecdotal reports too often found in the literature. It is that need for rigorous study that this book addresses.

The ibstpi Board acknowledges that many of those who function as instructors do not do so as a full-time job. Others do, and move easily from course to course. It is ibstpi's intention that all of the full- and part-time instructors in their various roles will benefit from the competencies and discussion presented here. This book does not address content-specific competencies; that is, the competencies and performance statements are applicable to those teaching any subject to any group of learners, whether they are in a face-to-face, online, or blended setting. The standards in this book have emerged from a thorough, worldwide understanding about learning, instruction, setting, and technology.

Furthermore, it is the Board's intention that this book has several audiences. Instructors can use it for self-evaluation, reflection, and professional development. Managers, department chairs, and supervisors can use it to evaluate instructor performance. Those who train instructors can use it for curriculum development, performance assessment, and certification.

Please visit the Board's website at http://www.ibstpi.org for more information about ibstpi.

—Timothy Spannaus
Wayne State University
Barbara Grabowski
Pennsylvania State University

Timothy Spannaus, Ph.D. is Senior Lecturer of Instructional Technology and Research Fellow in the Institute for Learning and Performance Improvement at Wayne State University. He served as a board member (1995–2004) and president of ibstpi (1999–2003). Barbara Grabowski, Ph.D. is Professor of Education in the Instructional Systems program at Pennsylvania State University and serves as the current ibstpi president.

ACKNOWLEDGMENTS

Many people and organizations contributed to the development of the instructor competencies described in this book. In addition to members of ibstpi, three Research Associates contributed in many significant ways: Radha Ganesan (Syracuse University), Hae-Deok Song (Pennsylvania State University), and Vickie Stout (University of Tennessee). We owe many thanks to Radha who was an ibstpi Research Associate assigned to the instructor competency development team for most of this project; she helped the Board retain the history of the effort while contributing to the exploration of competencies for online instructors. Hae-Deok helped analyze data and provided a critical examination of the updated instructor competencies compared with the 1993 competencies.

Several other individuals also contributed to this research and development effort: Cécile Égou and Karin Lundgren-Cayrol of Télé-université in Montréal helped in identifying relevant research literature, Meng-Fen Hsieh and Maria Moran at Pennsylvania State University helped with the initial data collection effort, and Xuemei Wang at Syracuse University helped with the development of the Web-based data collection instrument and in notifying potential respondents. Julie Hall at Syracuse University developed and deployed the Web-based instrument used to collect data for the validation study. Michael Harris at Arizona State University performed the initial statistical analysis of these data.

We offer special thanks to the organizations that co-hosted ibstpi meetings devoted to the development of these competencies, including:

- Arizona State University (Educational Technology Program, Tempe, Arizona)
- Centre for the Study of Advanced Learning Technology at Lancaster University (CSALT, Lancaster, United Kingdom)

Instructor Competencies: Standards for Face-to-Face, Online, and Blended Settings, pages xix–xx
Copyright © 2004 by Information Age Publishing
All rights of reproduction in any form reserved.

- EPISE Group (Barcelona, Spain)
- ERIC Clearinghouse for Information and Technology (Syracuse, New York)
- LICEF Research Center at Télé-université (Montréal, Canada),
- Motorola, Inc. (Berlin, Germany)
- National Aerospace Laboratory (NLR, Amsterdam, The Netherlands)
- Syracuse University (Instructional Design, Development and Evaluation Program, Syracuse, New York)

Additionally, a number of professional associations helped us conduct the validation study and/or provided forums for discussion and presentation of initial findings:

- Academy of Human Resource Development
- Association for the Advancement of Computing in Education (Ed-Media, E-Learn)
- Association for Educational Communications and Technology (AECT)
- American Society for Training and Development (ASTD)
- Canada's Advanced Internet Development Organization (Canarie, Tele-learning)
- International Federation for Training Development Organizations (IFTDO)
- International Society for Performance Improvement (ISPI)
- International Forum for Instructional Technology (ITFORUM)

Furthermore, individual Board members contacted many colleagues and organizations to discuss various aspects of the instructor competencies. These individuals and organizations are too numerous to list but their contributions are greatly appreciated.

Finally, we would like to thank the more than 1,300 respondents to the lengthy data collection instrument for their help in defining these competencies and the numerous individuals with whom various Board members have engaged in lengthy and productive discussions about the nature of teaching and learning.

CHAPTER 1

AN INTRODUCTION TO INSTRUCTOR COMPETENCIES

OVERVIEW

When asked to name someone who impacted their life, many people include an instructor on their list. Instructors who make an impact have special qualities that make them memorable; they also possess a wealth of knowledge, skills, and attitudes that make them competent. This book focuses on competencies for instructors as identified and validated by the International Board of Standards for Training, Performance and Instruction (ibstpi).

The mission of ibstpi is to develop, validate, and promote the implementation of international standards to advance training, instruction, learning, and performance improvement for individuals and organizations. The Board has identified and validated competencies for instructional designers (Richey, Fields, & Foxon, 2001), training managers (Foxon, Richey, Roberts, & Spannaus, 2003), and recently completed a 4-year effort to update our competencies for instructors.

The original set of ibstpi instructor competencies mainly addressed the standards for trainers in face-to-face classroom settings (see Appendix A). They have been used as the foundation for the certification of technical trainers and as the basis for many train-the-trainer programs. The recently updated ibstpi instructor competencies reflect developments in teaching and learning in the past decade and the use of online and blended delivery

Instructor Competencies: Standards for Face-to-Face, Online, and Blended Settings, pages 1–11
Copyright © 2004 by Information Age Publishing
All rights of reproduction in any form reserved.

systems. In addition, they have been validated globally with a sample of more than 1,300 practitioners in all regions of world.

Our main purpose in writing this book is to make the updated ibstpi instructor competencies available to the field and to describe how they can be applied in face-to-face, online, and blended settings. Our aim is to help instructors facilitate learning and improve performance of individuals and organizations. Throughout the book, the job title of instructor will be used to refer to individuals who are responsible for activities intended to improve skills, knowledge, and attitudes. In some organizations and cultures, other titles such as trainer, facilitator, teacher, or tutor are used to describe this job. Our intent in this book is to be comprehensive and our focus is on all those who actively and directly support learning and performance.

Another purpose of the book is to recommend how individuals and organizations can use the competencies for professional development, selection and hiring, performance appraisal, and as the basis for curriculum development and certification tests. In addition, we explain the process followed by ibstpi to develop competencies and present the results of an empirical study we conducted to validate the updated competencies for instructors. Below, we provide the foundation for the updated ibstpi competencies by discussing the evolution of instructor competence.

THE EVOLUTION OF INSTRUCTOR COMPETENCE

In order to provide a foundation for the updated ibstpi instructor competencies, this section addresses two central questions:

- How have people conceptualized the relevant knowledge, skills and attitudes required in order to be an effective instructor?
- How have these skills, knowledge and attitudes changed over time?

The first question is basic to any exploration of instructor competence. Addressing it will provide a point of reference and help determine the general nature of what is being discussed in this book. The second question is motivated by recent changes in teaching and learning as well as significant developments in the use of technology in education and training.

Traditional Conceptualizations of Instruction

What does it mean to be an instructor? This apparently simple question opens a window to a myriad of perspectives on teaching and learning. Instruction takes many forms and is related to the culture and context in which it takes place. In tribal cultures, passing knowledge, skills, and attitudes from one generation to the next is based on a variety of activities, including demonstration and storytelling. In some cases, a young learner observes an elder hunting an animal or weaving a basket or planting crops and gradually is included in these activities. In other cases, an elder or tribal leader would gather a group and tell stories to preserve knowledge and tradition. In some Asian cultures, this question leads to the concept of a guru or sensei. In this tradition, the instructor has recognized competence in some specialty (e.g., calligraphy, dance, martial arts) and passes this competence along to others who observe and practice under the master's supervision.

In addition to indicating the historical richness of teaching and learning, these examples provide an essential aspect of being an instructor, which is the purposefulness of activities intended to promote learning and performance. In a broad sense, an instructor intentionally helps others develop knowledge, skills, and attitudes. In order to better understand how instructors are able to succeed, two western traditions—didactic and apprenticeship—are examined below. This discussion concludes with a more complete context for instructional competencies.

Socrates is often cited as an example of a good instructor with the Socratic method as an exemplar of effective instruction. The popular recollection of Socrates is that he challenged listeners with probing questions and often revealed inconsistencies in their thinking, forcing those with whom he spoke to abandon previously held positions and consider alternative positions. Many educators believe that the Socratic method of questioning is effective because it seems to promote reflective and critical thinking. There is evidence to suggest that providing opportunities for reflection is conductive to learning, especially when what is to be learned is relatively challenging (Dörner, 1996).

Some also argue that the Socratic method of teaching is consistent with and a good example of learner-centered instruction. On a one-to-one basis, Socrates tried to help individuals examine their thoughts, identify inconsistencies, and develop a deeper understanding of such complex notions as goodness and virtue. Socrates cared about people and what they thought. He focused his attention on individuals. In this sense, Socrates's instruction was learner-centered. This is somewhat different from the modern emphasis placed on learner-centered instruction in which learners are challenged to construct their own interpretations of and solutions to problems (Duffy & Cunningham, 1996; Jonassen, Hernandez-Serrano, & Choi, 2000). Socrates believed that the problems he addressed had only one correct solution because these problems involved eternal truths about external realities, such as the fundamental nature of virtue and the good life.

Socrates's method of instruction was quite unique. He engaged individuals in almost any setting and used whatever objects were at hand to illustrate concepts. The Socratic method was oral and informal. Socrates engaged individuals on a voluntary basis, and often these individuals were prominent youth and leading citizens.

Socrates existed at the same time that another didactic instructional tradition developed, namely the Sophist tradition. The Sophists were recognized as especially well-informed on a broad range of subjects, and they usually charged a fee for their instruction. The Sophists taught in a more formal manner than Socrates did, and they did not generally apply the Socratic questioning method. The Sophists taught in one-on-one settings and in small groups, but the learners went to a particular learning place to receive instruction. The Sophists focused on instructing prominent youth and leading citizens. They planned lessons and made use of documents and concrete objects from nature.

The Sophist tradition might be regarded as the precursor of a major instructional approach to teaching—namely, the didactic approach (sometimes less affectionately called the sage-on-the-stage approach). This approach to instruction is usually associated with an instructor lecturing on a subject with students listening respectfully. The traditional didactic approach to instruction in classroom settings has a number of advantages, including efficiencies associated with having many people meet in one place at the same time. Moreover, when the instructor is a well-informed, accomplished speaker and when learning outcomes are appropriately supported with lecture methods, the motivation to learn can be high and desired learning outcomes attained. Nevertheless, there are limitations to the didactic approach to instruction, which is best used to support cognitive and social skills rather than psychomotor skills.

The apprenticeship model stands in sharp contrast to the didactic approach. While there is the potential to realize economies of scale and other efficiencies using the didactic approach and lectures, the apprenticeship model is a one-on-one method that aims to promote the development of refined skills and deep understanding of a narrow set of ideas. The apprenticeship model was developed during the Middle Ages with the rise of a class of citizens associated with trades and crafts. These skilled workers would train a small number of associates who would assist them and often take over the shop when the owner died or retired. The period of apprenticeship was long and involved a great deal of supervision by the master craftsman. This method of training has evolved into standard practice in a number of vocations and professions that involve periods of internship or apprenticeship prior to certification.

Whereas the primary occupation of a Sophist was instruction, the primary occupation of a master craftsman was the production of goods and services with instruction integrated into everyday working activities. In the apprenticeship model, the tools of the trade are an integral part of the instruction; mastering the use of a particular tool is often the focus of instruction. Learners are trained in the workshop using established and stable procedures applied to actual tasks. The instructional style and method varied with the individual instructor; both the method of production and the method of instruction passed from master to apprentice. This approach is similar to on-the-job training (OJT) methods used by many organizations today.

What was the impact of these approaches to instruction? One might be tempted to conclude that the didactic approach is well suited to support the acquisition of declarative knowledge (facts and concepts) whereas the apprenticeship approach is best suited to support the acquisition of procedural knowledge (applying rules and principles). Such a conclusion oversimplifies the teaching–learning situation. In *Integrative Goals for Instructional Design*, Gagné and Merrill (1990) argued that it is typical to have multiple objectives and multiples types of learning involved in a single unit of instruction. There are multiple and interconnected objectives involved when learning such things as troubleshooting a device or designing an improved space shuttle part. People want to understand how economies behave in reaction to external political events or how to improve the environmental quality of a local region or why terrorism appears to be worsening, and so on. What people want and need to learn has changed in the last 50 years. Have these changes resulted in new learning paradigms that then call for new approaches to instruction and new instructor competencies? Have new technologies and tools that evolved during the same period introduced a need for new approaches to teaching and new instructor competencies? The next two sections of this chapter address these questions.

New Learning Paradigms

Several writers have argued that learning has changed dramatically in the last 50 years (cf. Spector & Anderson, 2000). Goodyear (2000) focuses on changes in learners and argues that they are much less compliant than in previous generations. This is partly a consequence of extending learning opportunities to adults in the workplace and elsewhere. These adults have legitimate educational interests and requirements and they constitute a new group of nontraditional learners who exist primarily outside the traditional classroom setting. Goodyear characterizes these learners as noncompliant and quite different from compliant learners who sit and listen respectfully. Noncompliant learners generally have well-defined goals and concerns, and they have a wealth of life experiences beyond the classroom.

To expect such learners to adopt easily or quickly to the lectures used in the didactic approach may not be realistic and may result in suboptimal learning or in driving these nontraditional learners away.

Jonassen and colleagues (2000) argue that a different approach to instruction is required on account of an entirely new learning paradigm. This paradigm suggests that:

- People construct internal representations of external realities.
- Internal representations are interpreted constructions of reality; they are sometimes shared with and understood by others.
- Knowledge is built up from these representations.
- The quality of active learning experiences is related to the effectiveness of instruction.

These ideas have implications for instruction, including such things as providing multiple ways to represent knowledge (Spiro, Coulson, Feltovich, & Anderson, 1988), providing more support for novice learners (Collins, Brown, & Newman, 1989), and asking learners to engage in explicit model-representation activities with their peers (Milrad, Spector, & Davidsen, 2000).

The existence of new types of learners and new approaches to instruction warrants another look at instructor competencies. How does an effective instructor manage such learners? How does an effective instructor take into account differences in existing knowledge that impacts how new knowledge is internally represented and constructed? The competencies described later in this book address these important questions.

The standard definition of learning remains largely unchanged, however. Cognitive science has contributed to our understanding of how learning occurs and how learning may best be supported, but learning still involves changes in a person or a group of people. Learning involves stable and persisting changes in knowledge, skills, and attitudes. These changes are manifested in observable ways. This notion is fundamental to assessing learning outcomes and, therefore, in determining the effectiveness of instruction.

New Educational Technologies

Milrad and colleagues (2002) noted that:

Technology changes. Technology changes what we do and what we can do. People change on account of technology. Technology in support of learning and instruction is no different. Instructional technology changes what teachers and learners do and can do. (p. 13)

Many new technologies have been introduced in the last 50 years, including an explosion of new information and communications technologies building on the successes of the personal computer and the Internet. What impact are these new technologies having on instruction?

First, educational technologists should be honest and admit that many new technology innovations have been oversold and many of the promises of improved learning based on new technologies have not been kept (Spector, 2000). Educational television did not replace the teacher. Computer-assisted learning did not make classroom instruction unnecessary. Web-based instruction is not resulting in dramatically improved learning outcomes.

Second, it should be recognized that new technologies do provide new ways to support learning and opportunities for different kinds of learning activities. There are more ways to communicate than previously possible or affordable, thanks to new information and communications technologies (ICT). Students can interact with each other using a variety of digital technologies such as chat, threaded discussions, Internet-based network meetings, text messaging, and so on, in addition to agreeing to meet for coffee after class. Instructors can likewise engage in a greater variety of communication modes with students and other participants in the teaching–learning setting. Moreover, many of these digital modes of communication provide a record of what was said by whom and on what occasion. Such information can be used to monitor learning progress and to improve the overall communication support for learning. The competencies presented later in this volume address these new forms of communications.

New technologies provide more than support for new forms of educational communication. Electronic devices and interactive simulations can be used to promote learning and performance. In some cases, these can be designed to engage remotely located learners. Digital or virtual environments in which learners can formulate and test hypotheses can be used to promote understanding of such complex domains as environmental management and medical diagnosis (Milrad et al., 2002).

Paquette (2002) has identified six different models for integrating these new technologies into instruction. Three models focus on the instructor: (1) an instructor and learners in a common location with computers connected to the outside world; (2) an instructor and learners located in different places and connected via ICT with asynchronous interactions; and (3) an instructor and learners located in different places and connected via ICT with synchronous interactions. Paquette's other three models place most of the responsibility on the learner with the instructor acting primarily as a manager.

The settings in which learning occurs are being altered dramatically by new technologies, and this has implications for instructor competencies.

The boundaries between working and learning are not always clear as in the case of the apprenticeship model and with modern electronic performance support systems (Spector & Wang, 2002). What instructors do in these new settings is often quite different as well. The next section addresses these changes.

NEW ROLES AND SETTINGS FOR INSTRUCTORS

When ibstpi embarked on this enterprise of updating instructor competencies, it was evident that there was a need to account for new tools, settings, and roles due to emerging technologies and to the renewed emphasis placed on learner-centered instruction. What new settings and tools do instructors encounter and what new roles are required? The answer varies with the setting in which instruction takes place. Three different settings are discussed next: face-to-face, online, and blended environments. Face-to-face settings include classrooms and apprenticeship situations such as OJT. Online settings are interpreted very broadly, and include both synchronous and asynchronous environments that involve technologies such as video-conferencing, chat and instant messaging, threaded discussions, Web-based course management systems, and so on. Blended settings refer to learning environments that include a mixture of face-to-face and online situations. In addition to the instructional roles for these various settings, instructors are often required to interact with others such as instructional designers, training managers, subject matter experts, technicians, system specialists, as well as other instructors.

Face-to-Face Settings

The traditional classroom has not disappeared, nor is that likely to happen. Face-to-face settings have distinct advantages, such as the instructor's ability to react to nonverbal cues and the ability of an instructor or learner to react immediately to a group. Learners and instructors are familiar with and generally comfortable in face-to-face settings. Furthermore, negotiation between learners and an instructor can be conducted efficiently. A face-to-face setting allows the same message to be delivered simultaneously to many students who can then ask for clarification and listen to each other's responses. On the other hand, a classroom setting does not easily lend itself to private conversations, individualized instruction, or time-independent reflection.

Classrooms are being transformed by technology in a variety of ways, as noted by Paquette (2002). Moreover, classrooms with computers can function as laboratory environments. Deciding how to use technology in the classroom is a major issue confronting instructors at all levels. The question is not whether or not to allow technology in the classroom. The issues that arise concern are how best to do this with fairness to all learners, how to match a particular technology to a particular learning task, and how to be sure that technology is being used to promote learning and performance rather than becoming the focus of the learning activity.

In addition to the integration of new technologies, learner-centered instructional activities are being used more often in classroom settings (Klein, 2002). These activities allow learners opportunities to interact with each other and to have more freedom of choice than offered in the past. Instructors in face-to-face settings require knowledge and skills related to these active learning strategies and new technologies. The updated ibstpi instructor competencies reflect these skills and knowledge.

Online Settings

Some instructors find themselves in situations where the learners are remotely located, perhaps at many different places, none of which is in a classroom. The online setting that most closely resembles a traditional classroom is that established through video-conferencing. In some cases, there are both local and remote learners; in some cases, there are multiple sites involved. The temptation of an instructor in such a setting may be to behave as if it were a traditional lecture setting. This often turns out to be a mistake. If the instructor is used to pacing back and forth, the movement can create a disturbance for the remotely located learners and create other technical difficulties such as variable audio quality or jerky movements. Worse than the technical problems, however, is the fact that remotely located learners in such a setting may have a different social context without a local instructor and will most likely react differently to the lecture. New lecturing skills are required in such settings (Goodyear, Salmon, Spector, Steeples, & Tickner, 2001; Spector & de la Teja, 2001)

When the online setting involves a Web-based course management system, threaded discussions often become a primary and important learning activity. Students often require guidance in how to interact in such asynchronous discussion settings. The skills required to facilitate threaded discussions are quite different from those required in face-to-face settings. A similar argument can be made with regard to synchronous chat sessions. Both students and instructors require new skills to effectively engage in meaningful chat sessions. As yet, there are few training programs aimed at the development of such instructor skills. The ibstpi instructor competencies provide a foundation upon which such training programs might be constructed.

Blended Settings

Blended or hybrid settings are those that make use of a variety of instructional settings, including some aspects of face-to-face and online instruction. Blended settings are gaining in popularity in situations where face-to-face courses now have supporting websites and Web-based activities. In addition to the skills required for classroom and online settings, those instructors who find themselves in blended settings need to be able to decide when and which technology or tool to use for a particular learning activity. They also require the additional skill of being able to help students make adjustments from one setting to another. The set of competencies elaborated in this book provide the foundation for the development of these important instructor skills.

CONCLUSION

This chapter began with two questions: (1) How have people conceptualized the relevant knowledge, skills, and attitudes required in order to be an effective instructor? and (2) How have these skills, knowledge, and attitudes changed? Being an instructor has traditionally been conceptualized in terms of face-to-face settings in either a classroom or an apprenticeship situation. Teaching now involves the use of apprenticeship methods and approaches in the classroom and may involve online situations that require entirely new skills. In fact, one can think of all instructional settings as blended settings if they are conceived broadly to include instructional settings with a variety of methods, strategies, tools, technologies, and delivery techniques.

A definition of an instructor based on the Socratic model was that an instructor was someone who reminded others of things they had forgotten. A more modern point of view is that an instructor is a voice—sometimes a voice that is heard but sometimes one that is virtual. An instructor is the eye that reflects—sometimes the eye that detects a disengaged student and poses a challenge and sometimes a virtual eye that must guess if someone is disengaged and requires assistance. An instructor is the hand that guides – sometimes this is a physical hand demonstrating how to do a particular thing but sometimes this is a virtual hand that suggests trying a different approach. An instructor is the face that does not turn away—the face that learners expect to see and hear and listen and reply. Sometimes this is a physical face but can be a virtual face; the listening and replying are nevertheless important.

In one sense, good instruction is good instruction regardless of the setting. While instruction has undergone many changes over the centuries, some core competencies have remained intact. These include the ability to communicate effectively and establish credibility with learners. Instruction is an intentional activity that involves planning, preparation, management, and the application of sound methods and strategies. Effective instructors are able to discern when things go well and when they don't and adjust accordingly.

The competencies in this book apply to instructors in face-to-face, online, and blended settings. They take into account the requirements introduced by new learners, new technologies to support learning and performance, and new approaches to instruction. While it is difficult to identify everything a capable instructor should know and do, the ibstpi instructor competencies are comprehensive and can be applied in many teaching and learning settings throughout the world.

CHAPTER 2

THE IBSTPI COMPETENCY DEVELOPMENT MODEL

OVERVIEW

In the previous chapter, we discussed how instructor competence has changed over time and described several instructional approaches and settings. In general, being an instructor has become more complex and challenging over the years as a result of increased knowledge about human learning, new information and communications technologies and the effects of globalization. In this chapter, the focus is on the ibstpi competency development model and how it was applied to identify and validate the instructor competencies. This model was developed by ibstpi and has proven useful and robust in the development of competencies for instructional designers (Richey et al., 2001), training managers (Foxon et al., 2003), and the instructor competencies presented in the next chapter.

WHAT IS A COMPETENCY?

Most definitions of competency development involve supporting or improving human performance. According to Richey and colleagues (2001), a *competency* describes the critical ways in which competence is demonstrated; competence is the state of being well qualified. Lucia and Lepsinger (1999) define a competency as the knowledge, skill, or characteristic

Instructor Competencies: Standards for Face-to-Face, Online, and Blended Settings, pages 13–21
Copyright © 2004 by Information Age Publishing
All rights of reproduction in any form reserved.   13

required to effectively perform a role in an organization. Parry (1998) identifies a competency as knowledge, attitudes, or skills that define the core abilities required for successful performance in a given job. McLagan (1997) suggests that competencies can be viewed in six different ways: (1) job tasks; (2) results of work efforts; (3) outputs; (4) knowledge, skills, and attitudes; (5) qualities that describe superior performers; and (6) bundles of attributes. Similarly, Hooghiemstra (1992) defines competencies as "motives, traits, self-concepts, attitudes or values, content knowledge, or cognitive or behavioral skills—any individual characteristic that can be measured or counted reliably and that can be shown to differentiate significantly between superior and average performers, or between effective and ineffective performers" (p. 28).

The International Board of Standards for Training, Performance and Instruction (ibstpi) defines competency as:

> A set of related knowledge, skills, and attitudes that enable an individual to effectively perform the activities of a given occupation or job function to the standards expected in employment.

As defined by ibstpi, competency is related to performance on a job and can be measured against commonly accepted standards. This approach combines several points of view concerning competencies including a collection of knowledge, skills, and attitudes, an identification of job tasks, and the qualities of superior performers that can be measured reliably (Hooghiemstra, 1992; Lucia & Lepsinger, 1999; McLagan, 1997; Richey et al., 2001; Parry, 1998). The ibstpi competencies are statements of performance, not personality traits or beliefs. Furthermore, there is an implication that competence can be developed through training and instruction.

THE COMPETENCY DEVELOPMENT MODEL

Competency development models are used to identify required knowledge, skills, attitudes, capabilities, and job tasks within a defined occupation or organizational role. According to Marrelli (1998), "a competency model is the organization of identified competencies into a conceptual framework that enables the people in an organization to understand, talk about, and apply the competencies" (p. 10).

Figure 2.1 illustrates the ibstpi competency development model. Competency development begins with a well-defined job role. If a well-defined job role does not exist, then defining it becomes the initial step. As indicated in Chapter 1, there are many people with various job titles who support learning and who are responsible for activities intended to improve

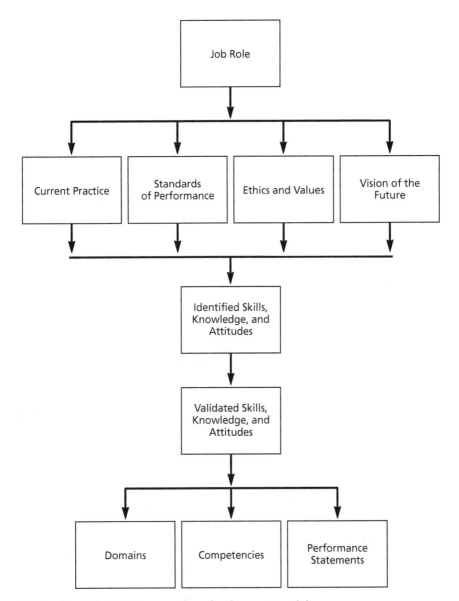

Figure 2.1. The ibstpi competency development model.

skills, knowledge, and attitudes. All of these individuals are considered instructors from the ibstpi perspective. As a consequence, this competency development effort began with a broad conception of being an instructor. Lucia and Lepsinger (1999) indicate that job roles can be defined generically or they can be customized to reflect a specific work environment.

While the ibstpi competencies relate to a particular job role such as *instructor,* they reflect a more generalized view of an instructor's job. Therefore, a specific position within any organization may relate to only a portion of these competencies.

The ibstpi competency development model includes three phases (see Figure 2.1). The first phase focuses on identifying current practice, expected standards of performance, ethics and values, and a vision of the future. The second phase focuses on identifying the knowledge, skills, and attitudes associated with competent performance and then validating the competencies. In the third and final phase, validated competencies are elaborated using more detailed performance statements and are clustered into related domains of activity. This three-phase process is iterative and should be repeated when a job role has changed sufficiently to warrant an update of competencies. This is the case with the ibstpi instructor competencies.

Once a job is defined, specific current practice and existing standards are identified to facilitate competency development. Furthermore, the ethics and values commonly used to evaluate such behaviors must also be determined. Finally, a future vision of the job role is clarified. This vision may be the result of emerging trends and interpretations of current research, or it may be the result of societal or business pressures. Current practice, existing standards, ethics, values, and future vision all provide the major input into the identification and validation of the knowledge, skills and attitudes critical to a particular job role (Foxon et al., 2003; Richey et al., 2001).

The ibstpi competency model consists of three important components: domains, competencies, and performance statements (see bottom of Figure 2.1). A domain is a cluster of related competencies. Each domain categorizes a group of competencies into an area of activity and identifies a theme for that cluster. Spencer and Spencer (1993) recommend this tactic for competency modeling. The five domains we identified for the ibstpi instructor competency model are: Professional Foundations, Planning and Preparation, Instructional Methods and Strategies, Assessment and Evaluation, and Management.

Competency statements are the central component of the ibstpi model. Each one is a short, general description of a complex effort. One example from the Instructional Methods and Strategies domain is "Demonstrate effective questioning skills." Like all competencies, additional detail is required to more fully explain what is involved in demonstrating effective questioning skills. These explanations are provided via performance statements. Demonstration of a particular competency consists of several specific performances. For example, the competency for demonstrating effective questioning is partially supported by the performance statements, "Ask clear and relevant questions" and "Use questions to generate and guide discussions." Competencies and performance statements are structurally the same, differing only in the level of detail and behavior specificity.

APPLYING THE MODEL TO INSTRUCTOR COMPETENCIES

The ibstpi competency development model provided direction for the identification and validation of competencies for instructors in face-to-face, online, and blended learning settings. The specific process used to update the instructor competencies was an empirical approach that was implemented over a 4-year period. The major phases of this approach are described below.

Phase 1: Review of Literature and Practice

The 1993 ibstpi instructor competencies served as a foundation for the current set of competencies and performance statements. In addition, literature that focused on recent developments in teaching and learning and on the use of online and blended delivery systems was reviewed. We examined the standards for online instruction in response to requests from industry, academia, and the field. Furthermore, materials from several train-the-trainer courses offered in corporate and educational settings were examined to discover current instructional practices.

These sources led to a revised list of instructor competencies that included more than the 14 competencies in the 1993 set, which confirmed the Board's belief that instructor roles had undergone significant change in the last 10 years. Initially, the Board was focused primarily on online instruction in response to expressed interest in competencies for this setting. The Board decided to update competencies for face-to-face settings while developing a new set of competencies for online settings. After examining the evidence developed in the first year, the Board came to the conclusion that competencies for online instructors were not substantially different from competencies for instructors in face-to-face settings and the competency development effort should proceed accordingly. Over a period of time, instructors are likely to be required to teach in settings that involve a variety of technologies and instructional approaches (i.e., blended settings).

Phase 2: Competency Identification and Validation

The ibstpi Board, in collaboration with the Centre for the Study of Advanced Learning Technology at Lancaster University in the United

Kingdom, hosted a meeting of international scholars and practitioners with expertise in teaching and learning in online settings in June 2000 in Windermere, England. These experts began to identify the knowledge, skills, and attitudes for online teachers and tutors and also suggested that there was a great deal of similarity with competencies for instructors in face-to-face settings (see Goodyear et al., 2001). In addition, the ibstpi Board served as an expert panel throughout Phase 2 that analyzed and debated the revised instructor competencies. Board members with particular expertise in a given area revised initial competencies and performance statements. These revised statements were analyzed, debated, and rewritten several times to reflect input from the board and outside experts and to establish consistency of format and language.

A validation instrument was developed, pilot tested, and administered after the revised list of instructor competencies and performance statements had the unanimous approval of the ibstpi Board. The instrument asked respondents to rate the criticality of each competency and performance statement for instructors in face-to-face and online settings and to comment on each statement. Respondents included instructors, trainers, teachers, designers, and managers from diverse geographic locations and organizations. Individuals rated the criticality of statements in a particular setting only if they had teaching experience in that setting. The instrument also included a demographic section to gather information about respondents (see Chapter 6 for a detailed description of the validation study).

Phase 3: Competency Revision and Final Approval

Data obtained from over 1,300 individuals who participated in the validation study were analyzed to determine which statements were perceived as critical for instructors in face-to-face and online settings. Statements that were not clear were also identified in this phase. Having responses for face-to-face and online settings allowed the Board to assess its decision to treat instructor competencies as generic and generally applicable for blended settings. This decision is strongly supported by the data, which indicate that these instructor competencies can be applied in a wide variety of settings.

In nearly all cases, the final list of competencies included statements that received a rating of 4.0 or above on a 5-point scale for both face-to-face and online settings. Open-ended comments made by respondents were used to revise statements for meaning and clarity. These revised statements were again analyzed, debated, and rewritten to reflect input from survey respondents and board members. The ibstpi Board unanimously approved the final list of instructor competencies presented in this book.

ASSUMPTIONS ABOUT
THE IBSTPI INSTRUCTOR COMPETENCIES

The updated competencies are based on some assumptions about the nature of instruction and the function of competencies for instructors. The assumptions discussed below influenced the identification, development, and validation of the competencies and may influence their interpretation and use.

Assumption 1: The goal of instruction is to facilitate learning and improve performance. The competencies discussed in this book focus on the knowledge, skills, and attitudes that enable an individual to perform effectively in the role of an instructor. Many of the competencies provide a description of the processes and tactics used by skilled instructors. However, we think it is important to point out that the goal of effective instruction is to facilitate learning and improve the performance of individuals and organizations. Instructors, therefore, have an obligation to apply these processes and use these tactics to assist learners and organizations to develop and change.

Assumption 2: Instructors are individuals responsible for activities intended to improve knowledge, skills, and attitudes, regardless of their specific job title. The updated competencies are applicable for individuals whose job encompasses enhancing learning and improving performance. The ibstpi Board made the decision to continue to use the job title of *instructor* for these updated competencies. We recognize that other titles such as *facilitator, teacher, trainer,* or *tutor* are used in some organizations and cultures. We believe that the ibstpi instructor competencies are relevant for all these professionals regardless of their specific job title, including those occasionally engaged as instructors, as is the case with many on-the-job trainers.

Assumption 3: Instructor competencies apply to a wide range of settings and instructional approaches. These updated competencies identify a standard set of skills that effective instructors should possess. While instructors who work with adult learners are the primary audience for these competencies, they can be applied to a variety of instructional settings. We think that effective instructors should have these competencies whether they teach in face-to-face, online, or blended settings. As already noted, the Board began this effort thinking that instructor competencies for online and face-to-face settings would be significantly different but was soon convinced based on a substantial body of evidence that this was not the case. We also believe that these competencies apply to trainers and facilitators in business, industry, government, and public service settings as well as to teachers and tutors in academic and school environments.

Assumption 4: Factors such as instructional setting, organizational practice, and local culture influence the application of instructor competencies. Even though the competencies are relevant to a range of instructors and settings, several factors affect how they are applied in practice. For example, tutors in online environments and trainers in classroom settings should be proficient in making presentations, facilitating groups, asking questions, giving feedback, and using technology. However, the ways in which these instructors demonstrate their competence will differ due to the setting and culture in which they work (see Chapter 4 for a detailed discussion of how the competencies can be demonstrated in different settings). In addition, the degree to which an instructor is responsible for planning methods and materials or evaluating instructional effectiveness depends on the organization in which he or she works.

Assumption 5: Few individuals demonstrate all of the instructor competencies, regardless of their level of expertise and amount of education or training. These instructor standards are comprehensive; the list includes 18 competencies supported by 98 performance statements. The extensive nature of these competencies makes it unlikely that an instructor will demonstrate every knowledge, skill, and attitude included in the list. Even those with substantial work experience and extensive education or training should be able to use these competencies to identify areas for improvement and professional development.

Assumption 6: Competent instructors are responsible for more than the delivery of information and content. The comprehensive nature of the competencies also indicates that an effective instructor assumes a variety of roles and responsibilities. While some individuals are not responsible for the design of instructional materials, all competent instructors plan and prepare in advance of an instructional assignment. Furthermore, they are capable of implementing strategies to facilitate learning, assessing learner performance, evaluating the effectiveness of instruction, using technology, and managing the processes and people in an instructional setting.

Assumption 7: Instructor competencies should be meaningful and useful worldwide. The Board has made a conscious effort to develop competencies that are valuable to practitioners working in many countries and cultures. This is accomplished by using terminology that can be understood in multiple languages and by making each competency and performance statement free of cultural bias. The updated instructor competencies described in this book were written with the input of individuals who have lived and worked in Africa, Australia, Asia, Europe, North America, and South America. Furthermore, they were validated by a sample of practitioners from diverse geographic locations around the world. Additionally, the instructor competencies have been translated from English into a number of languages, including Catalan, Chinese, French, Japanese, Korean, Spanish, and Ukrainian (see http://www.ibstpi.org).

CONCLUSION

The ibstpi competency development model has been successfully used to identify and validate competencies for instructional designers, training managers, and now instructors. This chapter has examined the model and how it was applied to the job role of instructor. The next chapter provides a complete list of the updated ibstpi instructor competencies and performance statements followed by a chapter that illustrates how they can be implemented in face-to-face, online, and blended instructional settings.

CHAPTER 3

THE IBSTPI INSTRUCTOR COMPETENCIES[1]

OVERVIEW

This chapter provides a list of the ibstpi instructor competencies and performance statements. They represent a significant update to the instructor standards previously published by ibstpi. The updated list includes 18 instructor competencies clustered in five general domains and supported by 98 performance statements.

The updated instructor competencies and performance statements reflect developments in teaching and learning in the past decade and the use of online and blended delivery systems. They have been validated globally with a sample of more than 1,300 practitioners in all regions of the world (see Chapter 6). These instructor standards reflect the core competencies of instructors—the knowledge, skills, and attitudes that competent instructors typically demonstrate. The competencies and performance statements define the generic skills of an instructor independent of setting and organization. Competent instructors will possess these standards whether delivering face-to-face instruction to a large audience or facilitating an online discussion with a small group of learners. The domains, competencies, and performance statements are given below.

Instructor Competencies: Standards for Face-to-Face, Online, and Blended Settings, pages 23–28
Copyright © 2004 by Information Age Publishing
All rights of reproduction in any form reserved.
23

PROFESSIONAL FOUNDATIONS

Competency 1: Communicate effectively.

  (a) Use language appropriate to the audience, context, and culture.
  (b) Use appropriate verbal and nonverbal language.
  (c) Seek and acknowledge diverse perspectives.
  (d) Use active listening skills according to context.
  (e) Use appropriate technology to communicate.

Competency 2: Update and improve one's professional knowledge and skills.

  (a) Expand one's knowledge of learning principles and instructional strategies.
  (b) Continuously update technology skills and knowledge.
  (c) Establish and maintain professional contacts.
  (d) Participate in professional development activities.
  (e) Document one's work as a foundation for future efforts.

Competency 3: Comply with established ethical and legal standards.

  (a) Recognize the ethical and legal implications of instructional practices.
  (b) Comply with organizational and professional codes of ethics.
  (c) Ensure that learners are treated fairly.
  (d) Respect requirements for confidentiality and anonymity.
  (e) Avoid conflicts of interest.
  (f) Respect intellectual property including copyright.

Competency 4: Establish and maintain professional credibility.

  (a) Model exemplary professional conduct.
  (b) Respect the values and opinions of others.
  (c) Demonstrate subject-matter expertise.
  (d) Be open to change and improvement.
  (e) Relate instruction to organizational contexts and goals.

PLANNING AND PREPARATION

Competency 5: Plan instructional methods and materials.

  (a) Determine relevant characteristics of learners, other participants, and instructional settings.
  (b) Plan or modify instruction to accommodate learners, instructional settings, and presentation formats.

(c) Identify and sequence goals and objectives.

(d) Select appropriate instructional methods, strategies, and presentation techniques.

(e) Plan or modify lessons, instructor notes, assessment tools, and supporting materials.

(f) Create or modify technology-based resources as required.

Competency 6: Prepare for instruction.

(a) Anticipate and prepare for learner difficulties and questions.

(b) Prepare learners for instruction.

(c) Identify key points, relevant examples, anecdotes, and additional materials.

(d) Confirm logistical and physical arrangements that support instruction.

(e) Make instructional resources accessible to all learners.

(f) Confirm readiness of equipment, technology, and tools.

INSTRUCTIONAL METHODS AND STRATEGIES

Competency 7: Stimulate and sustain learner motivation and engagement.

(a) Gain and maintain learner attention.

(b) Ensure that goals and objectives are clear.

(c) Foster a favorable attitude toward learning.

(d) Establish relevance to increase learner motivation.

(e) Help learners set realistic expectations.

(f) Provide opportunities for learners to participate and succeed.

Competency 8: Demonstrate effective presentation skills.

(a) Adapt presentations to the learning context.

(b) Represent key ideas in a variety of ways.

(c) Provide examples to clarify meaning.

(d) Involve learners in presentations.

(e) Adapt presentations to learner needs.

Competency 9: Demonstrate effective facilitation skills.

(a) Draw upon the knowledge and experience of all participants.

(b) Give directions that are clearly understood by all learners.

(c) Keep learning activities focused.

(d) Encourage and support collaboration.

(e) Bring learning activities to closure.

(f) Monitor, assess, and adapt to the dynamics of the situation.

Competency 10: Demonstrate effective questioning skills.

- (a) Ask clear and relevant questions.
- (b) Follow up on questions from learners.
- (c) Use a variety of question types and levels.
- (d) Direct and redirect questions that promote learning.
- (e) Use questions to generate and guide discussions.
- (f) Build on responses to previous questions in subsequent learning activities.

Competency 11: Provide clarification and feedback.

- (a) Provide opportunities for learners to request clarification.
- (b) Use a variety of clarification and feedback strategies.
- (c) Provide clear, timely, relevant, and specific feedback.
- (d) Be open and fair when giving and receiving feedback.
- (e) Provide opportunities for learners to give feedback.
- (f) Help learners in giving and receiving feedback.

Competency 12: Promote retention of knowledge and skills.

- (a) Link learning activities to prior knowledge.
- (b) Encourage learners to elaborate concepts and ideas.
- (c) Provide opportunities to synthesize and integrate new knowledge.
- (d) Provide opportunities to practice newly acquired skills.
- (e) Provide opportunities for reflection and review.

Competency 13: Promote transfer of knowledge and skills.

- (a) Use examples and activities relevant to application settings.
- (b) Demonstrate the application of knowledge and skills in realistic settings.
- (c) Provide opportunities to practice in realistic settings.
- (d) Provide opportunities to plan for future application.
- (e) Explore with learners the conditions that may help or hinder transfer.
- (f) Provide opportunities for autonomous learning.

Competency 14: Use media and technology to enhance learning and performance.

- (a) Recognize the capabilities and limitations of media and technology for instruction.
- (b) Apply best practices when using media and technology.
- (c) Represent content in a variety of ways.
- (d) Prepare learners for the use of media and technology.
- (e) Troubleshoot or fix minor technical problems.

ASSESSMENT AND EVALUATION

Competency 15: Assess learning and performance.

(a) Communicate assessment criteria.
(b) Monitor individual and group performance.
(c) Assess learner attitudes and reactions.
(d) Assess learning outcomes.
(e) Provide learners with opportunities for self-assessment.

Competency 16: Evaluate instructional effectiveness.

(a) Evaluate instructional materials.
(b) Evaluate instructional methods and learning activities.
(c) Evaluate instructor performance.
(d) Evaluate the impact of the instructional setting and equipment.
(e) Document and report evaluation data.

MANAGEMENT

Competency 17: Manage an environment that fosters learning and performance.

(a) Anticipate and address situations that may impact learning and performance.
(b) Ensure that learners can access resources.
(c) Establish ground rules and expectations with learners.
(d) Employ time management principles during instruction.
(e) Discourage undesirable behaviors in a timely and appropriate manner.
(f) Resolve conflicts and problems quickly and fairly.

Competency 18: Manage the instructional process through the appropriate use of technology.

(a) Use technology to support administrative functions.
(b) Use technology to seek and share information.
(c) Use technology to store and reuse instructional resources.
(d) Use technology to maintain the security and privacy of learner information.

The next chapter provides the rationale for these competencies and performance statements and indicates how they can be demonstrated in a variety of face-to-face, online, and blended settings. The following chapter describes how various individuals and organizations can use the competencies and how they can be applied to instructor certification.

NOTE

1. The ibstpi instructor competencies and performance statements are copyrighted by the International Board of Standards for Training, Performance and Instruction (ibstpi). All rights reserved.

CHAPTER 4

INSTRUCTOR COMPETENCIES

Discussion and Rationale

OVERVIEW

This chapter examines the ibstpi instructor competencies and performance statements.[1] Each section includes: (a) an overview of the competencies in a particular domain, (b) a description of each competency and how it is supported by related performance statements, and (c) a discussion of how specific performance statements can be demonstrated in face-to-face, online, and blended instructional settings. The chapter is organized around five competency domains, each of which represents a related set of knowledge, skills, and attitudes associated with various instructor activities and tasks. These five domains are: (1) Professional Foundations, (2) Planning and Preparation, (3) Instructional Methods and Strategies, (4) Assessment and Evaluation, and (5) Management. The following sections provide an explanation of the competency and performance statements in each domain.

PROFESSIONAL FOUNDATIONS

The competencies in the Professional Foundations domain are an explicit recognition that instructors are members of a profession with responsibili-

Instructor Competencies: Standards for Face-to-Face, Online, and Blended Settings, pages 29–58
Copyright © 2004 by Information Age Publishing
All rights of reproduction in any form reserved.   29

ties that extend beyond the teaching–learning setting. As with any profession, there are obligations and expectations for instructors related to effective communication, improving one's own knowledge and skills, complying with legal and ethical principles, and maintaining credibility. The knowledge, skills, and attitudes required to fulfill these obligations and expectations comprise the professional foundations of teaching or training.

Each of the competencies discussed below are supported by four to six performance statements that address the knowledge, skills, and attitudes that are relevant to the demonstration of that instructor competency.

Competency 1: Communicate effectively.

(a) Use language appropriate to the audience, context, and culture.
(b) Use appropriate verbal and nonverbal language.
(c) Seek and acknowledge diverse perspectives.
(d) Use active listening skills according to context.
(e) Use appropriate technology to communicate.

Effective communication is a fundamental skill for every instructor. The data on which this set of competencies is based indicate that communication skills are considered by practicing professionals to be the most critical skills of an effective instructor (see Chapter 6). A competent instructor regularly communicates with many different individuals and groups including learners, tutors, instructional designers, subject-matter experts, training managers, support staff, and other instructors. A capable instructor also uses a variety of means to communicate, including face-to-face meetings, memoranda, telephone calls, e-mail messages, and audio- and videoconferences.

Appropriate language is dependent on the audience, context, and culture in which the communication occurs. For example, informal language, incomplete sentences, and "emoticons" (special characters used as shorthand to express emotions) may be appropriate to use in e-mail messages and chats in some contexts, while other situations require more formal communication styles. Establishing expectations and rules of engagement for electronic communication ("netiquette") is often helpful, especially when learners from several different cultures are involved and when face-to-face meetings are not possible.

The appropriate use of nonverbal language is another important skill for an instructor. A competent instructor in a face-to-face setting effectively uses tone of voice, eye contact, gestures, silence, movement, posture, and space during a presentation to enhance communication (Hutchison, Shepherd, & Stein, 1988). However, it should not be assumed that skill in nonverbal communication only applies to face-to-face settings. For example, AN INSTRUCTOR IN A TEXT-BASED ONLINE SETTING WHO USES

ALL CAPITAL LETTERS (FOLLOWED BY A SERIES OF EXCLAMATION POINTS) TO RESPOND TO QUESTIONS FROM LEARNERS HAS NOT MASTERED THE APPROPRIATE USE OF NONVERBAL LANGUAGE!!! Of course it is sometimes appropriate to use capital letters for emphasis in an online setting, just as it is occasionally appropriate to raise one's voice in a face-to-face setting.

While using active listening is also context specific, this skill can be applied in all teaching–learning settings, especially when listening is understood to include attending to all perceptual cues. A competent instructor is expected to listen carefully, convey to the speaker (or writer) that the instructor is listening, paraphrase comments and questions from learners to show understanding, and separate learners' feelings from their comments to correct errors or misconceptions without being demeaning or insulting to learners (Collison, Elbaum, Haavind, & Tinker, 2000; Hutchison et al., 1988; Ko & Rossen, 2001). Principles of active listening can be applied in a variety of settings, including classrooms where an instructor and learners are physically present, teleconferences where only the spoken word can be heard, and online courses where communication may occur asynchronously or synchronously via written messages and graphics as well as real-time and streaming audio and video. For example, an instructor using videoconferencing technology employs active listening by nodding or using other body language to let the learner know that the instructor is listening.

A competent instructor also uses appropriate technology to communicate. Knowing when and how to use video, audio, text, and graphics provides alternative communication channels to express ideas and allows instructors to tailor instructional messages to accommodate those with different communication skills and needs. In online settings, instructors have to choose the appropriate technology according to different criteria such as temporality (synchronous or asynchronous), the number of people communicating (dyads, triads, small groups, large groups, etc.), and the nature of communication (one to one, one to many, or many to many).

Competency 2: Update and improve one's professional knowledge and skills.

    (a) Expand one's knowledge of learning principles and instructional strategies.
    (b) Continuously update technology skills and knowledge.
    (c) Establish and maintain professional contacts.
    (d) Participate in professional development activities.
    (e) Document one's work as a foundation for future efforts.

Instructors are expected to engage in ongoing efforts to update and improve their professional knowledge and skills. A competent instructor keeps abreast of current principles of learning and instruction. Furthermore, knowledge and skill pertaining to the use of technology should be continuously updated, as changes in communication and delivery media frequently occur. Capable instructors update their skills for using new technology and devices and their knowledge about current research on the conditions and effects of technology on learning. Participation in professional development activities such as attending meetings of professional organizations, reading journals and trade magazines, and establishing and maintaining professional contacts can help an instructor be more effective. Technology allows instructors to also take part in virtual communities of practice, to subscribe to relevant forums and technology watch services, and to regularly access relevant websites and portals.

In addition to expanding one's own knowledge and skills, instructors are expected to document their work as a foundation for future efforts. This ranges from keeping notes for reflection and self-improvement to improving a particular instructional activity that did not work to making presentations at professional meetings and publishing articles to advance knowledge in the field.

Competency 3: Comply with established ethical and legal standards.

(a) Recognize the ethical and legal implications of instructional practices.
(b) Comply with organizational and professional codes of ethics.
(c) Ensure that learners are treated fairly.
(d) Respect requirements for confidentiality and anonymity.
(e) Avoid conflicts of interest.
(f) Respect intellectual property including copyright.

As a member of a profession, every instructor is obligated to comply with established ethical and legal standards of professional practice. The set of performance statements listed above makes this obligation explicit for instructors. These statements recognize that there are ethical and legal implications of instructional practice. In addition to formal laws and professional codes of ethics, many organizations have policies, guidelines, and standard procedures that govern the actions of their instructors. A competent instructor is aware of these guidelines and is expected to adhere to them.

Instructors in all settings are expected to comply with formal legal standards, professional codes of ethics, and organizational policies and guidelines. Respecting intellectual property including copyright is especially important given the increased use of the Web to deliver instructional materials and the ease with which such rights can be violated (Richey et al., 2001). Instructors who use technology must also be diligent to safeguard learner confidentiality and anonymity given the ease that private information can be electronically stored and retrieved. For example, an instructor with access to information such as passwords, access codes, personal information, and records must respect individual rights. In some cases, an online instructor must be aware of international rights or agreements among multiple organizations when learners come from different countries or from multiple organizations. Furthermore, instructors have a special obligation to comply with copyright, model appropriate behavior to learners, and ensure that documents are protected from illegal use. They also have a responsibility to be aware of legal practice related to the use of technology, including the authentication of a learner's identity through electronic signatures, photos, or other means.

The International Board of Standards for Training, Performance and Instruction has identified specific ethical standards pertinent to the work of instructors. These standards provide further explanation of ethical behavior for instructors and can be found in Appendix B. They relate to several areas of ethics including individual rights and responsibilities, social and organizational rights and responsibilities, and obligations to oneself as an ethical agent. In some areas such as intellectual property and privacy, ethical standards have some connection with legal requirements. The Board views legal requirements as setting the minimum standard for acceptable behavior in these areas whereas ethical guidelines are more broad in scope and aim toward a higher standard than that required by law.

Competency 4: Establish and maintain professional credibility.

  (a) Model exemplary professional conduct.
  (b) Respect the values and opinions of others.
  (c) Demonstrate subject-matter expertise.
  (d) Be open to change and improvement.
  (e) Relate instruction to organizational contexts and goals.

A competent instructor must intentionally establish and maintain professional credibility. An instructor who works with adult learners does not automatically gain credibility because he or she is in a position of authority. Credibility depends on being perceived as knowledgeable in the subject domain and open to new ideas and approaches. Regardless of setting or delivery system, an instructor must be credible in order to facilitate learning and performance.

There are several aspects of professional credibility for instructors, including personal credibility, social credibility, and content credibility

(Hutchison et al., 1988). An instructor with personal credibility models exemplary professional conduct. This includes accepting responsibility in the teaching and learning setting, respecting start and ending times, admitting personal mistakes and ignorance, and presenting a personal appearance in a way that is appropriate to the audience and setting. For example, appearance in an online setting is partially established by the initial welcome message and the instructor's signature. It also means inviting and accepting feedback about one's performance as an instructor and being open to change and improvement.

An instructor with social credibility respects the values and opinions of others. Skilled instructors establish and maintain an atmosphere of respect and trust. They respect individuals regardless of their age, appearance, sex, race, culture, disability, learning style, or other distinguishing characteristic. A capable instructor avoids the use of questionable humor and stories that demean another individual's gender, culture, ethnicity, or sexual orientation. The appearance of favoritism and bias is also avoided.

Finally, an instructor with content credibility demonstrates subject-matter expertise. A competent instructor has mastered instructional content and can answer questions accurately, thoroughly, and confidently. A credible instructor also can relate instruction to organizational contexts and goals. Knowing how to make use of the knowledge and skills involved in the instruction is an essential part of content credibility.

PLANNING AND PREPARATION

Successful instruction requires planning and preparation. A competent instructor plans or modifies lessons, strategies, and activities prior to implementing them. This requires collecting information about learners and the instructional setting in order to select or modify methods and materials. A skilled instructor also must prepare before leading learning activities or delivering instruction to learners. Preparation involves readying oneself, as well as learners, materials, and equipment.

The two competencies discussed below recognize the importance of advance planning and preparation. Six performance statements that indicate the skills, knowledge, and attitudes in the Planning and Preparation domain support each competency.

Competency 5: Plan instructional methods and materials.

(a) Determine relevant characteristics of learners, other participants, and instructional settings.

(b) Plan or modify instruction to accommodate learners, instructional settings, and presentation formats.

(c) Identify and sequence goals and objectives.

(d) Select appropriate instructional methods, strategies, and presentation techniques.

(e) Plan or modify lessons, instructor notes, assessment tools, and supporting materials.

(f) Create or modify technology-based resources as required.

The degree to which an instructor is responsible for planning instructional methods and materials varies depending on several factors, including organizational practice and specific job responsibilities. Some instructors are primarily responsible for implementing courses developed by an instructional designer within the organization or by an outside vendor. In these settings, an instructor may follow an instructor guide as written or modify an instructional activity based on knowledge about learners or past experience when teaching the course. In other organizations, an instructor is responsible for both the design and implementation of instructional methods and materials. In these contexts, the instructor assumes the role of an instructional designer and may be responsible for determining organizational and learner needs, identifying course objectives, and developing instructional materials and assessments.

The competency and performance statements for planning instructional methods and materials are not intended to replace those for instructional designers. An instructor who is frequently required to design instruction should have the skills, knowledge, and attitudes discussed in *Instructional design competencies: The standards* (Richey et al., 2001).

Many instructors are not responsible for the design of instruction. However, skilled instructors should be able to determine the relevant characteristics of learners, other participants, and instructional settings. They also know how to plan or modify instruction to accommodate these characteristics and presentation formats. Skilled instructors are able to anticipate changes that are likely to occur in an instructional situation and adapt accordingly. For example, an instructor in an online setting may be asked to teach an existing course with learners and tutors from a number of different countries and cultures. This may require knowing the abilities of learners to write, talk, and work at a distance as well as their previous experience with online collaboration. An instructor might have to plan new strategies for learner, tutor, and instructor interaction in advance of implementing a course. As the course progresses, the instructor might have to modify those strategies. Online and blended settings have opened new opportunities for individual, personalized learning. A competent instructor can adapt according to their learners' progress.

A competent instructor should also be able to select and adapt appropriate instructional methods, strategies, and presentation techniques. For example, an instructor in a blended setting might be required to plan both face-to-face and online sessions that take the unique nature of both settings into account. A skilled instructor who teaches in face-to-face settings should consider strategies and presentation techniques other than standard lecture approaches to meet the requirements of a particular situation.

A capable instructor also can create or modify technology-based resources as required. While the level of expertise for this performance will vary from instructor to instructor, it ranges from modifying existing presentation materials for a face-to-face lecture to creating an online course using the latest authoring tools. In online settings, the instructor may need to frequently modify some resources; for example, questionnaires or forms that have been completed or modified by one group of students in an online environment may need to be revised and uploaded before another group can use them.

Competency 6: Prepare for instruction.

   (a) Anticipate and prepare for learner difficulties and questions.
   (b) Prepare learners for instruction.
   (c) Identify key points, relevant examples, anecdotes, and additional materials.
   (d) Confirm logistical and physical arrangements that support instruction.
   (e) Make instructional resources accessible to all learners.
   (f) Confirm readiness of equipment, technology, and tools.

A competent instructor is prepared before delivering instruction. Content, activities, materials, equipment, and learners all require preparation. An instructor with prior knowledge about learners identifies potential questions and content that might be difficult, and determines what information and examples should be emphasized. A prepared instructor examines activities before implementing them to determine how much time is required for the activity, what materials and services are required, and what problems might occur. In online settings, preparing and or consulting previous FAQs (lists of frequently asked questions with answers) may be useful for instructors. In addition, instructors must also be prepared to deal with problems related to technologies used in the instructional setting.

The degree to which an instructor prepares learners for instruction, makes resources accessible, and confirms logistical arrangements and equipment readiness varies depending on organizational context and individual job responsibilities. Some instructors have staff to assist with these tasks while other instructors are responsible for making sure that participants are registered, a location is arranged, and equipment or technology resources are obtained. Successful instruction requires that these tasks be completed regardless of who in the organization is responsible for them. A competent instructor knows how to ensure that these tasks are successfully completed.

These activities also vary in face-to-face, online, and blended instructional settings. For example, placing cameras and microphones in strategic places are essential in settings using videoconferencing to ensure proper visibility and audibility for all participants. In addition, an instructor teaching a Web-based course might have to ensure that learners have access to online resources such as a company database or school library as well as human resources such as content experts, technicians, and other members of the community of practice. It is also important to make all documents accessible to every participant. Preparing learners in online and blended settings may include ensuring they possess the adequate technical skills and knowledge and principles of collaboration as well as the fundamentals of self-management. Furthermore, an instructor could also prepare learners for online instruction by sending a motivating e-mail message before the actual course begins (Visser, Plomp, Amirault, & Kuiper, 2002). While instructors in face-to-face settings also prepare learners for instruction, it is more usual for this to occur at the start of the course rather than beforehand.

Instructors in all settings also confirm readiness of equipment, technology, and tools. This may range from readying flipcharts and projection devices in face-to-face settings to determining the usability and functionality of hyperlinks and remote control devices in online and blended settings. Regardless of setting, a competent instructor ensures that equipment, technology, and tools are ready before instruction begins.

INSTRUCTIONAL METHODS AND STRATEGIES

The primary goal of instruction is to improve learning and performance. Competent instructors use a variety of methods and strategies to reach this goal. For example, an instructor should be able to make effective presentations, facilitate teamwork, ask clear and relevant questions, and provide timely feedback. Furthermore, a capable instructor knows how to motivate learners and how to support retention and transfer of newly learned skills.

The Instructional Methods and Strategies domain includes eight competencies that are at the center of an instructor's responsibility. Each competency in this domain is supported by five to six performance statements that clarify what is involved in the activity.

Competency 7: Stimulate and sustain learner motivation and engagement.

(a) Gain and maintain learner attention.
(b) Ensure that goals and objectives are clear.
(c) Foster a favorable attitude toward learning.
(d) Establish relevance to increase learner motivation.
(e) Help learners set realistic expectations.
(f) Provide opportunities for learners to participate and succeed.

Establishing and maintaining learner motivation is one of the most important responsibilities of an instructor. Motivation is prerequisite to learning and performance (Gagné, 1985; Gagné & Medsker, 1996). It influences the choices people make and how much effort they exert (Keller, 1983). While learners come to an instructional setting with different needs and motives, most adults want to succeed, share their ideas, participate, and have their contributions recognized (Knowles, Holton, & Swanson 1998).

A competent instructor uses a variety of strategies to stimulate and sustain learner motivation. The performance statements that support this competency provide detail to show how an instructor can address learner motivation. However, they are not intended to be an exhaustive list of motivational strategies. Instructors looking for more ideas about how to motivate learners may refer to Keller (1987) for an extensive list of strategies to address attention, relevance, confidence, and satisfaction or to Wlodkowski (1998) for strategies to enhance adult motivation.

Instructors in face-to-face, online, and blended settings are expected to address learner motivation and engagement. However, the feeling of isolation that some online learners experience (Grabowski, Suciati, & Pusch, 1990) suggests that instructors in these settings must continually provide opportunities for learners to participate and succeed (Collison et al., 2000). Instructors in online settings may face a particular challenge when it comes to fostering intrinsic motivation because some learners may perceive online learning as being of less value than learning in face-to-face settings (Cook & Timmis, 2002). Another misconception that can hinder motivation is that online learning requires less effort than face-to-face learning. It is thus important for the instructor to foster favorable attitudes towards online learning by highlighting the inherent opportunities of those settings.

On the other hand, given all the possibilities offered by online settings, learners may have unrealistic expectations such as unlimited instructor availability or complete personalization of learning. This may result in a decrease in motivation if the instructor does not help learners set realistic expectations. Instructors need to provide strategies allowing online learners to know the limits and advantages of the technology and how to use it to attain their objectives. Furthermore, they should help learners develop an accurate view of the effort required to succeed in an online and blended setting.

Competency 8: Demonstrate effective presentation skills.

(a) Adapt presentations to the instructional setting.
(b) Represent key ideas in a variety of ways.
(c) Provide examples to clarify meaning.
(d) Involve learners in presentations.
(e) Adapt presentations to learner needs.

The capability to make effective presentations is another important skill for instructors in all settings. It should not be assumed that effective presentation skills are only appropriate for instructors in face-to-face settings who use the lecture method. Instructor presentations also can be offered via audio, video, text, and graphics. Competent instructors should know and apply principles of effective electronic presentations. Moreover, a competent instructor can adapt a presentation to the setting and to learner needs. This means that the instructor should have some knowledge of effective screen design principles.

Regardless of the setting, an effective presentation focuses learners on important points by representing key ideas in a variety of ways. This can be accomplished by using animations, illustrations, diagrams, schematics, models, sounds, and concrete objects. Online presentations have to take into account that excessive animation can be distracting and that long texts may be difficult to read on the screen. A competent presenter uses examples, anecdotes, stories, analogies, and humor effectively. They also involve learners in presentations by including time for questions, discussion, and reflection.

Effective presenters establish contact with learners. Instructors in face-to- face settings accomplish this by making eye contact with participants, by varying the range and volume of the voice, by pausing to emphasize important points, and by using gestures, movement, posture, space, and props effectively (Hutchison et al., 1988). In an online setting, it is especially important for instructors to establish a sense of presence. For example, an instructor in an asynchronous setting recognizes learner contributions, addresses learners by name, and sends messages to nonparticipating learners. In a synchronous videoconference, an instructor establishes and maintains presence by asking questions of learners at specific locations, looking at the instructor camera, and speaking clearly into the microphone.

Competency 9: Demonstrate effective facilitation skills.

   (a) Draw upon the knowledge and experience of all participants.
   (b) Give directions that are clearly understood by all learners.
   (c) Keep learning activities focused.
   (d) Encourage and support collaboration.
   (e) Bring learning activities to closure.
   (f) Monitor, assess, and adapt to the dynamics of the situation.

In addition to making effective presentations, a competent instructor demonstrates effective facilitation skills. An effective facilitator monitors, assesses, and adapts to the dynamics of a teaching–learning setting. This is accomplished by using attending, observing, listening, and questioning skills. Attending skills are used to pay attention to learner needs and concerns. Observing skills are used to assess how learners are receiving an instructional activity and to decide whether to continue the activity as planned or modify it. Listening skills are used to obtain information and feedback from learners and to demonstrate an understanding of their concerns, questions, and comments. Questioning skills are used to involve learners and to determine whether they are learning.

An effective facilitator draws upon and uses the knowledge and experiences of all participants. Participants typically consist of learners and the instructor, but may include others such as tutors and technical assistants in online and blended settings. Discussion and collaboration is used to allow participants to share experiences and to learn from each other (Flynn & Klein, 2001; Klein & Doran, 1999). A competent instructor encourages and supports collaboration among all participants. Furthermore, an instructor facilitates by seeking and sharing information and ideas among participants with diverse backgrounds.

Effective facilitation means that an instructor provides clear directions when introducing and explaining an activity and keeps learning activities focused. Effective facilitation also means that an instructor brings activities to successful closure. This is accomplished when newly acquired skills and knowledge are meaningfully linked to learning objectives. Techniques for keeping activities on track include reminding learners of objectives, asking learners to summarize, tracing the progress of a discussion, and making observations that time is limited or that a learner or a group is on the right or wrong track. To do so in online settings, instructors can monitor a student's navigation path. For example, it is possible to analyze learner patterns as well as to verify the coherence of threads of discussions in forums and e-mail messages. In asynchronous activities, the instructor can keep learning activities focused by addressing messages that deviate from the activity goal to different forums or by connecting them to other discussions. One of the challenges for an online instructor is to weave together and make sense of various comments and discussion threads.

Given that learners are distributed in online settings, an effective instructor needs to put in place the tools and the strategies to collect and analyze knowledge from learners at a distance, and then make it accessible to all participants. Encouraging collaboration in online settings may include tools and strategies to evaluate and foster the cohesion and productivity of the group (Henri & Lundgren-Cayrol, 2001). Among those tools is an online list of participants, a presentation card for each participant (indicating their goals, interests, how to contact them, etc.), and a virtual space for socializing.

Competency 10: Demonstrate effective questioning skills.

(a) Ask clear and relevant questions.
(b) Follow up on questions from learners.
(c) Use a variety of question types and levels.
(d) Direct and redirect questions that promote learning.
(e) Use questions to generate and guide discussions.
(f) Build on responses to previous questions in subsequent learning activities.

An instructor who asks effective questions gives participants an opportunity for active involvement in the teaching–learning process. An effective question is clear, pertinent, brief, and challenging (Eitington, 1996). According to Beary (1994), questions have several purposes—to serve as an icebreaker, to assess knowledge and attitudes, to deflect antagonism, to link one topic to another, and to facilitate team development. Questions can also be used to get participants to clarify a response or think more deeply, to generate and guide discussions, to manage groups, and to deal with problem behaviors.

A variety of question types and levels can be used to promote learning. Types include open, closed, direct, indirect, reversed, redirected, and probing questions (Hutchison et al., 1988; Suessmuth & Strengels, 1972). Levels include knowledge, application, reflection, evaluation, and synthesis questions (Anderson & Krathwohl, 2001). A capable instructor directs and redirects questions to facilitate learning. Questions are directed to promote wide participation among learners. The number, difficulty, and complexity of questions should match the learner's level of understanding and an adequate amount of time should be provided for a response to be made. Questions are redirected, repeated, rephrased, or restructured when an incorrect or incomplete response is given. Learners who give incorrect or incomplete responses are guided toward correct and complete responses; correct portions of partially correct answers are acknowledged and used in a constructive manner (Hutchison et al., 1988).

A competent instructor demonstrates effective questioning skills regardless of the teaching–learning setting. However, some differences exist between face-to-face and online settings. The amount of time between asking a question and getting responses in an asynchronous setting will typically be longer than in a classroom or in a synchronous chat room. Managing responses to questions in a synchronous online setting can be difficult when several learners post their answers at the same time. Furthermore, an instructor in an asynchronous setting may find it difficult to follow up on questions from a large number of learners, especially when private e-mail is used to communicate. In these situations, electronic bulletin boards can be used to post responses to frequently asked questions and other participants such as tutors may be employed to interact with learners. On the other hand, online technology facilitates follow-up of questions asked by an individual and allows forwarding of the question to the rest of the group or to other human resources. In online settings, instructors may include hyperlinks in their questions and ensure relation with other learning activities. Frequently, online learners generate questions relative to technical problems, in which case it is important for the instructor to redirect them to the right resource and make sure that they have been answered.

Competency 11: Provide clarification and feedback.

　(a)　Use a variety of clarification and feedback strategies.
　(b)　Provide clear, timely, relevant, and specific feedback.
　(c)　Provide opportunities for learners to request clarification.
　(d)　Be open and fair when giving and receiving feedback.
　(e)　Provide opportunities for learners to give feedback.
　(f)　Help learners in giving and receiving feedback.

Providing clarification and feedback to students helps to facilitate their learning and improve their performance. Clarification can alleviate difficulties, minimize misunderstandings, and eliminate misconceptions. Feedback provides learners with guidance and direction by correcting errors in performance or by reinforcing appropriate performance. Clarification and feedback can increase student interest, confidence, and effort.

An effective instructor is able to recognize when learners require clarification (Hutchison et al., 1988). While some learners feel comfortable asking for clarification, others are unwilling to indicate that they don't understand something. An instructor must be aware of and look for signs that a learner requires clarification. Cues such as a lack of involvement, attention, and comprehension help to identify students who require additional explanation. Instructors in face-to-face settings can use visual cues such as head nods and eye contact when trying to determine which students should receive clarification. In an online setting, instructors can examine comments made during threaded discussions and those posted on class discussion boards.

Instructors will be more effective if they explicitly integrate a variety of clarification strategies into their teaching (Anderson & Gipe, 1983; Barnitz, 1986; Simon, 1972). Clarification strategies include paraphrasing, providing analogies, and extending a concept or principle with a new example or application. Learners can also use these strategies effectively, and competent instructors encourage their students to do so.

Skilled instructors also use a variety of feedback strategies. These include providing verification and elaboration feedback (Kulhavy & Stock, 1989). Verification strategies provide confirmatory feedback thereby helping learners develop knowledge of their performance. Developing knowledge of performance involves providing feedback on a task plus information regarding the process used to perform or learn that task (Wallace & Hagler, 1979). Elaboration strategies provide corrective, informative, or reflective feedback (Dempsey & Sales, 1993). Reflective feedback can cause learners to pause and make choices or justify a response that was given. Competent instructors select from among these strategies based on the learning task and prior knowledge of the learner. For example, an effective feedback strategy for students with high prior knowledge who are learning a low-level cognitive task is to provide knowledge of the correctness or incorrectness of a response. On the other hand, when students have low prior knowledge or are learning a task that requires higher-order thinking skills, elaborative feedback should be provided (Dempsey & Sales, 1993; Kulhavy & Stock, 1989).

Feedback should be clear, timely, relevant, and specific. Clear feedback means that the instructor communicates the information in a way that is understandable to learners. Feedback should be tailored to the individual to make it relevant and specific to the task and to the learner. This means that feedback should be targeted to a particular performance rather than giving generic feedback. In most cases, feedback should be provided while the learner is performing a task or soon after a learner performs it. When dealing with psychomotor tasks, Romiszowski (1999) suggests that feedback *after* performance, rather than during performance, allows the learner to internalize the feel of the task.

One of the most challenging tasks related to feedback is to be open and fair when giving and receiving it. Being open means that the instructor shows a willingness to listen and consider learner justification for alternative responses. Fairness means that the instructor will treat all learners equally with dignity and respect when providing and receiving feedback. Because feedback may challenge an individual's self-esteem, it should be task-related, not personal.

Competent instructors provide opportunities for learners to give feedback to their peers and to the instructor. Peer feedback must be guided or framed to ensure appropriateness of the responses. Rubrics are especially helpful in framing peer feedback activities. Modeling appropriate feedback first or providing guided practice is also a useful strategy to direct the learners in this activity. In online synchronous discussions, the instructor should allow learners to give feedback at any time, providing them with the opportunity to raise their hand, react to the pace of the presentation (too fast, too slow), indicate their feelings or contentment (laughter, thumb down, applause), and show agreement or disagreement (by checking yes or no boxes).

Receiving feedback from learners is another important aspect of this competency. Adult learners bring rich experiences and backgrounds to a learning setting and can provide instructors with informed feedback on the task, the learning process, and the learning environment. A competent instructor is open to this feedback and responds in an accepting manner by becoming a participant in the learning situation. Feedback from learners can also help instructors improve activities, methods, and materials, as well as their own competencies.

Learners should also be given the opportunity to request feedback and clarification. When learners request clarification, they become aware of their progress toward mastering objectives, which promotes reflective practice (Schön, 1987). These opportunities shift the motivational strategy from external to internal approval (Gagné, 1985).

Feedback in a face-to-face setting can be provided with verbal responses or body language through a nod, smile, or glance. Providing feedback in an online setting can be particularly challenging to maintain an environment of openness and fairness. Instructors must be very selective in their choice of words to prevent being misunderstood. Brief or abrupt feedback in an online setting is easily misinterpreted as an angry reply. Online and blended settings also provide challenges and opportunities for providing a variety of feedback in a timely manner. To manage the workload, an instructor can create informal databases of responses that can be quickly tailored to an individual learner.

Learners in asynchronous settings can take time to reflect on feedback to their peers before providing it. However, given that the feedback can come from different sources, the online instructor needs to validate or verify the quality of the feedback.

To achieve the potential of feedback in online settings, instructors need to assess the appropriateness of using individual or group feedback. Some tools can hinder or facilitate the delivery and exchange of feedback and the instructor needs to know the limits and potential of them. As assignments completed by online learners can vary, providing feedback requires the instructor to use appropriate technology. For example, instructors should know how to insert a comment in a text or video file. They must also ensure that learners know how to interpret the comments and use the tools of technology. For example, learners must know how to use the *insert comment* or *track changes* features of a word processor if their instructor uses these tools. An effective strategy for providing continuous feedback in digital documents should be established. Moreover, given the importance of technology in online and blended settings, instructors need to be able to provide immediate feedback to technical problems in those settings as well as in face-to-face settings.

Competency 12: Promote retention of knowledge and skills.

(a) Link learning activities to prior knowledge.
(b) Encourage learners to elaborate concepts and ideas.
(c) Provide opportunities to synthesize and integrate new knowledge.
(d) Provide opportunities to practice newly acquired skills.
(e) Provide opportunities for reflection and review.

Skills and knowledge taught during instruction must be retained if they are to be used on the job or in life. An instructor can promote retention by linking new content to prior knowledge, by asking students to elaborate on to-be-learned concepts, and by giving learners a chance to practice newly acquired skills (Gagné, 1985). A skilled instructor can use a variety of strategies that encourage learners to generate relationships among concepts and between new ideas and their own prior understandings (Wittrock, 1974). Instructors can accomplish this by having students generate questions, objectives, summaries, graphs, tables, main ideas, concept maps, diagrams, and outlines. Instructors promote synthesis and integration in learners by having them create metaphors, analogies, examples, pictures, applications, interpretations, paraphrases, inferences, mnemonics, clarifications, and predictions (DiVesta, 1989; Jonassen, 1986; Wittrock, 1990). Note taking, creating diagrams, and constructing concept maps are appropriate for promoting both organizational and integrative thought.

A competent instructor also provides opportunities for reflection and review in order to enhance retention and promote higher-level learning. These activities relate new learning to prior knowledge by affording students an opportunity to think proactively about how much they have learned and which learning strategies work best for them (Atkins & Murphy, 1993; Boyd & Fales, 1983; Davis, 1998; Dewey, 1933; Moon, 1999;

Schön, 1991). An effective instructor uses a variety of strategies to prompt reflective thinking, including: (a) inquiry-oriented activities such as asking thoughtful questions, (b) explanation-oriented activities such as modeling thinking, and (c) scaffolding tools such as interactive journals and question prompts (Griffith & Frieden, 2000; Kinchin & Hay, 2000). Furthermore, a reflective learning environment is one that encourages learner decision making, exploration, and collaborative inquiry and requires students to justify and defend what they have learned (Duffy & Cunningham, 1996; Koszalka, Song, & Grabowski, 2002; Land & Hannafin, 1998; Williams, 1996). A competent instructor also employs wait time after asking questions and uses relevant tasks (Moon, 1999; Virtanen, Kosunen, Holmberg-Marttila, & Virjo, 1999).

Instructors in face-to-face, online, and blended settings can use these strategies because they are not media or location dependent. An instructor in an online setting can assign organizational, synthesis, or integration tasks that can be completed collaboratively and submitted electronically. An instructor in a blended setting can require students to meet online to reflect on what they are learning and doing in class. Online collaboration does not take away time from direct instruction like providing time for group work does in a face-to-face environment. Given that face-to-face time is not a factor in completing these tasks online, students can expend more thought in reflection and review.

Instructors in online and blended settings can direct learners to rich Internet resources that will help them elaborate new concepts and ideas. These instructors can use discussion boards to interject thoughtful questions to promote reflection and review. Instructors in online and blended settings can target reflective questions to specific students because of their ability to follow the flow of ideas and contributions by the entire group. In a face-to-face environment, the instructor can ask reflective questions that are selected based on a sense of the group obtained through visual and verbal cues from students.

In some online settings, it may be difficult for instructors to model thinking skills and to apply effective wait-time strategies. Face-to-face instructors can share their thinking in real time while demonstrating a task. Online instructors without video support must present these ideas using asynchronous methods or using a synchronous chat function. Instructors in face-to-face settings can use wait time by pausing several seconds to give students time to reflect on the question posed while instructors in a synchronous online environment might have to wait a few minutes to have the same effect. However, longer wait time is inherent in an asynchronous environment. An instructor must be able to discern between time for thinking and reflecting and a lack of student participation in a discussion; it typically takes an online instructor longer to make such determinations.

Competency 13: Promote transfer of knowledge and skills.

(a) Use examples and activities relevant to application settings.
(b) Demonstrate the application of knowledge and skills in realistic settings.
(c) Provide opportunities to practice in realistic settings.
(d) Provide opportunities to plan for future application.
(e) Explore with learners the conditions that may help or hinder transfer.
(f) Provide opportunities for autonomous learning.

In addition to promoting retention, effective instructors provide opportunities for learners to transfer new skills and knowledge to a job setting or to their lives. Strategies for promoting transfer range from using realistic cases and problems to selecting examples and activities from the setting where the new skills will be applied.

A competent instructor demonstrates the application of knowledge and skills and provides opportunities to practice in realistic settings. For realistic settings that have many distracting cues or events, such as an emergency room, the instructor can gradually increase the complexity of the situation so that the task, such as preparing a patient for an intravenous injection, is practiced initially by itself, then with all of the distracting cues of the real environment (Dwyer, 1978).

Learners should be given opportunities to create a plan for implementing newly learned skills back on the job. With this proactive plan, there is an increased likelihood that the learner will actually use new skills. The instructor provides a framework that enables the learner to consider the conditions that may hinder transfer and helps them plan for ways of countering them.

A skilled instructor concerned with transfer also provides students with opportunities for autonomous learning. They can ask students for personalized examples and problems from their job setting or other life experience to promote transfer. Instructors can gradually reduce the amount of prompting and feedback they give to students about task performance. In this way, responsibility for critical self-evaluation that will be required when returning to their job is gradually transferred to them.

Like other competencies, the capability to promote transfer is not media or location dependent and can be implemented by instructors in face-to-face, blended, or online settings. However, a skilled online instructor whose learners are taking their instruction at the workplace during the workday can create very realistic, timely, and relevant tasks that can be practiced, discussed, evaluated, and implemented on the job.

Competency 14: Use media and technology to enhance learning and performance.

(a) Apply best practices when using media and technology.
(b) Recognize the capabilities and limitations of media and technology for instruction.
(c) Represent content in a variety of ways.
(d) Prepare learners for the use of media and technology.
(e) Troubleshoot or fix minor technical problems.

In the hands of a competent instructor, media and technology can be used effectively to enhance learning and performance. Best practices for the effective use of media and technology include: (a) principles based on empirical research, (b) principles based on theory, (c) lessons learned from prior practice, and (d) established practice in a specific organization or local learning culture. In order to apply best practices in their own setting, instructors should keep current with regard to the use of existing, new, and emerging media and technologies (see Competency 2).

A skilled instructor uses a particular medium based on the requirements of the learning task, the content to be learned, the nature of specific learning activities, the messages to be conveyed, the characteristics of learners, and their location and local surroundings. Different media and technologies are used appropriately in different situations. Because media and technology may be expensive and may introduce additional complexity into the learning situation, a general guideline is to make use of media and technology in ways that are integral to specific learning activities rather than for cosmetic purposes. Enhancing learner motivation is integral to learning, and media and technology are often used effectively to enhance motivation.

Instructors who use text, images, audio, animations, video, computing, and communication media should take into account the capabilities and limitations of media and technology. Advances in technology may facilitate portability of digital files from one type of system to another, but in the meantime the instructor needs to consider the current limitations of media and technology. A skilled instructor who makes use of text to enhance a presentation uses white space effectively; appropriate font size for the setting; use of capitalization, italics, and underlining for emphasis; headings and questions for organization; and layout formats that can be scanned quickly (Hartley, 1985). An instructor also should take into account whether this text will appear on a learner's screen, a piece of paper, an overhead transparency, or a digital presentation when making such decisions. Instructors may use visuals to support motivation, organization, or integrative functions within a lesson; however, visuals that are irrelevant to the purpose of the lesson distract learners and should be avoided (Anglin, Towers, & Levie, 1996). Audio should be used when it is relevant to a task or to explain complex ideas or a demonstration; however, it should not be used as a voice synchronized with scrolling text, as this is known to interfere with learning (Barron & Atkins, 1994; Pavio, 1990). Animations and video can be used to enhance motivation, to demonstrate procedures and activities, and to draw attention to particular aspects of a learning task. However, too much motion in multiple places on a computer screen can be distracting and thereby detract from the instructional purpose.

The computer can be used as a communication medium in instruction. The skilled instructor uses the computer not only to present information but also to help learners organize, analyze, and synthesize information and to formulate hypotheses, make predictions, and make decisions (Pea, 1985). In an online or blended setting, the skilled instructor uses the Internet to bring in a variety of human and information resources that can increase relevance of learning tasks. Skilled use of the computer as a communication medium often requires effective moderation of online discussions (see Competency 9). This includes keeping discussions focused, handling inappropriate remarks tactfully but directly, generating useful discussions, involving everyone in discussions, introducing messages that link and relate remarks, and concluding with a synthesizing summary.

Technology and media enable an instructor to represent content and convey meaning in multiple formats to present information and provide motivation for a variety of different learners. Video may be used to accommodate learners who learn best through visual means; audio may be used to support those learners who learn best by listening; and tactile objects or manipulation of items on the computer may be used for kinesthetic learners. Specific media and enhancements might be required for individuals with disabilities. A skilled instructor also uses multiple formats and a variety of representations to help learners construct their own meaningful interpretations and representations, which is an effective way to reinforce learning (Spiro & Jehng, 1990).

A competent instructor will prepare learners to use media and technology for learning. Depending on the characteristics and prior experiences of learners, little technology preparation may be required for the use of video, audio, and text. However, the instructor should provide a context and an overview for the information students will see or use. The instructor needs to be ready to provide assistance for interpreting information conveyed through these media. A skilled instructor will direct learner attention to critical elements of a visual presentation. Although involving all learners is important in face-to-face classroom discussions, an instructor who uses audio or video-conferencing must be especially sensitive to engage learners in remote locations. A signal needs to be prearranged for learners in remote locations who have questions.

Instructors should prepare learners not to distract each other when using audio-conferencing. Specifically, participants should be reminded not to make extraneous noise and to identify themselves when providing comment. Skilled instructors who use technology for communication prepare their students by using effective moderating strategies, by helping learners understand the value of communicating with instructors and peers, by providing feedback as to the appropriateness of their responses, and by providing group and peer communication guidance (Salmon, 2000).

Preparing learners for using media and technology is critical in an online setting. Instructors should make sure that learners are comfortable with the technology to be used in order to concentrate on the learning objectives. A skilled instructor ensures that every student understands how to access and use the various communication and learning components of the instructional site. Prior to starting a course, an online instructor should provide practice tasks that require students to use these components and be available to help them be successful. Classroom instructors who integrate technology into their teaching and involve learners in using technology also have a responsibility to properly prepare learners for the use of technology.

Competent instructors are not required to be technical experts. However, they must be able to troubleshoot or fix minor technical problems such as burnt-out lightbulbs, make connection between computers and LCD projectors, and connect to the Internet when in a blended learning environment. In an online learning environment, technical problems arise that influence the motivation of learners. It is critical that instructors can either resolve the problems quickly themselves or direct the learners to technical support.

ASSESSMENT AND EVALUATION

The competencies in this domain suggest the importance of collecting information to assess learning and performance and to evaluate the effectiveness of instruction. Assessment provides information to learners and instructors about progress toward goals and objectives. It also helps instructors identify learners who may require additional instruction on a particular task before they are asked to apply their newly acquired skills on the job or in their life. Evaluation of methods, strategies, materials, and the instructor provides information to make teaching and learning more successful. The two competencies discussed below are both supported by five performance statements that help to define what makes an instructor competent in the Assessment and Evaluation domain.

Competency 15: Assess learning and performance.

(a) Communicate assessment criteria.
(b) Monitor individual and group performance.
(c) Assess learner attitudes and reactions.
(d) Assess learning outcomes.
(e) Provide learners with opportunities for self-assessment.

A competent instructor provides learners with the criteria for assessing outcomes at the time of assigning a task. Providing a scoring rubric is one way of clearly establishing these criteria, especially when learners are required to perform a difficult task. A skilled instructor will assess learning outcomes using assessment tools that match course objectives. If the objective is for learners to perform a skill, assessment should include an appraisal of performance. If the goal is for learners to adopt or modify an attitude, assessment should provide opportunities for choice and observation. If the goal includes learner participation, assessment criteria for quality and quantity should be communicated. Deadlines, scoring criteria, and how much each activity is worth should also be told to learners.

Frequently, it is important to monitor both individual and group learning and performance. Successful collaboration and teamwork requires that all members of a group are individually accountable for their own performance. It also means that team members have a reason for depending on each other and for working together toward the same goal. Competent instructors monitor group and individual performance. They also provide learners with the opportunity to assess their own individual performance and with a chance to monitor the progress of their team. Group members should also be given an opportunity to provide input on the performance of individuals on the team. To do so in online settings, it is possible to collect data by tracing learner paths individually or collectively. It is also possible in some systems to analyze how discussions and other activities are interleaved. Henri and Lundgren-Cayrol (2001) provide some ways to assess the cohesion of online groups.

Whether or not an instructor teaches in a face-to-face, blended, or online setting, assessment criteria should be established and communicated, student progress should be monitored, and learning outcomes should be assessed. Online and blended environments provide a good means for monitoring group progress though public and private group discussion forums. The competent instructor will be able to ascertain learner attitudes and reactions through comments posted to forums and bulletin boards. Online reflection tools that scaffold self-assessment also provide an efficient means for instructors to monitor progress.

Assessment poses some unique challenges for instructors who teach in online settings. It is difficult to monitor learner use of human and non-human resources during testing. The online instructor must also make sure that the person completing the assessment is the learner enrolled in the course. Assessment of psychomotor skills and other skills that require direct observation are particularly difficult in online settings. For example, participants in a fully online train-the-trainer course might be required to submit a videotape of their own teaching. This videotape would be scored using established criteria and elaborative feedback would be provided to participants.

Competency 16: Evaluate instructional effectiveness.

(a) Evaluate instructional materials.
(b) Evaluate instructional methods and learning activities.
(c) Evaluate instructor performance.
(d) Evaluate the impact of the instructional setting and equipment.
(e) Document and report evaluation data.

Four critical areas can impact instructional effectiveness: (1) instructional materials, (2) instructional methods and learning activities, (3) instructor performance, and (4) instructional setting, equipment, and infrastructure. These four areas function as a system, each influencing the other. When one area breaks down, instructional effectiveness can suffer. Therefore, a competent instructor will evaluate the effectiveness of all four areas during instruction and at the end of the instruction. Ongoing evaluation can help instructors monitor and adjust instructional effectiveness while end-of-course evaluation points to changes to future offerings.

Instructional materials should be evaluated for accuracy, relevancy, audience appropriateness, ability to communicate, and appropriateness of the medium. When technology is used, it should be evaluated for technical and mechanical functionality. Effectiveness, efficiency, and learner satisfaction should also be evaluated when technology is used. Instructional methods and learning activities should be evaluated to determine if they align with objectives and assessments. Methods and activities should also be evaluated to determine if they stimulate motivation, learning, and performance. Ongoing comments, difficulties, and complains posted by learners can be used by the online instructor to evaluate the materials.

Instructor performance is typically evaluated using a participant attitude survey. These surveys often measure such things as whether the instructor was clear, organized, interesting, likeable, and approachable. The ibstpi

Board thinks that instructor performance can and should be evaluated using the standards described in this book (see Chapter 5).

Finally, the impact of the instructional setting and equipment should not be underestimated. The setting and equipment should be evaluated for comfort and access to the information. These factors are equally important in face-to-face and online settings, although they may be interpreted differently. In a face-to-face environment, it is important that all learners be in a position to see the instructor, whereas in an online environment accessibility means learners have the appropriate technical capabilities (such as the browser, applets, power, and speed to access online course components) and are able to communicate with the instructor. In addition, tools for self-managing, conducting research, accessing documents, creating products, and collaboration should be evaluated. Evaluating online instructional materials may also require the instructor to have some knowledge of human-machine factors interaction, usability, and ergonomics in order to avoid unnecessary cognitive overload and stress due to poor interface design.

The degree to which an instructor is responsible for documenting and reporting evaluation data varies depending on several factors, including organizational practice and specific job responsibilities. However, a competent instructor will make sure that evaluation data are collected and used to improve instructional effectiveness. This ranges from taking notes to improve a particular learning activity to writing reports on the effectiveness of course methods and materials.

Valuable data can be collected to evaluate instructional effectiveness in online settings by using the audit trail functions of some learning management systems (LMSs). In some cases, the online instructor can use an LMS to be proactive and present questions requesting the learner's reactions during the learning process (Reeves & Hedberg, 2003). It is important in online settings to invite learners to indicate how they feel and to provide the means to express it. Their satisfaction toward the instructor, the materials, and the learning process in general is essential to measure the effectiveness of online instruction.

MANAGEMENT

In general, management involves supervising activities and making decisions to ensure that an enterprise operates as expected and achieves desired results. The goal of an instructional enterprise is to facilitate learning and improve performance. With regard to this enterprise, instructors are involved in key decision-making roles and are responsible for supervising the activities of learners. While management is not the primary function of an instructor, there are instructional processes, people, and environments for which the instructor is responsible. The two competencies in this domain reflect the primary management activities of an instructor. The Board has developed an entire set of competencies and performance standards for the training management function within an organization (see Foxon et al., 2003). The competencies discussed below are those involving the management of an instructional setting and the processes and technologies associated with that responsibility.

The competencies and associated performance statements in the management domain were not generally rated as high as those in other domains (see Chapter 6). However, the data do indicate that the management activities and responsibilities of instructors presented next are critical to the success of instruction. As before, there are notable differences in online and face-to-face settings.

Competency 17: Manage an environment that fosters learning and performance.

    (a) Anticipate and address situations that may impact learning and performance.
    (b) Ensure that learners can access resources.
    (c) Establish ground rules and expectations with learners.
    (d) Employ time management principles during instruction.
    (e) Discourage undesirable behaviors in a timely and appropriate manner.
    (f) Resolve conflicts and problems quickly and fairly.

Every instructional environment contains a number of resources; it is the instructor's ongoing responsibility to ensure that these resources are available and that learners can access them. The instructor is also responsible for establishing expectations and setting ground rules for interaction within a teaching–learning setting. Undesirable behaviors should be discouraged and dealt with in a timely and fair manner. Should conflicts or other problems arise, these should be resolved quickly and fairly. Anticipating problems and making appropriate adjustments in plans and processes in advance is a hallmark of a good instructor. Since online learning can take place in different locations throughout the world, an effective consideration of different time zones is often required, especially for facilitating synchronous discussions.

A common concern of instructors is that there is much to do, from planning and preparation to delivery and evaluation. A variety of resources and learning activities are often involved. Human interactions are also involved. Learners progress at different rates. Unanticipated situations arise. In order to be effective, a competent instructor must employ time management principles and strategies to govern the overall process as well as what happens with the learning environment during instruction.

There are obvious differences in these competencies for online and face-to-face instructors. In some organizations, face-to-face instructors do little to ensure access to resources other than ensuring that the door to a room is unlocked or that books are available in the library or bookstore. In other cases, face-to-face instructors do much more, including coordinating the copying and distribution of instructional materials. Often, online instructors confront a different situation that requires them to ensure that the learning environment is ready to use and that students enrolled in the course have access to the resources. An online learning environment often involves a variety of capabilities and functions, so this general requirement pertains to each component of the instructional system that is used.

Another difference in online and face-to-face instruction concerns the management of learning activities, especially those involving groups of learners. A common problem in online environments is for learners to fall behind, believing that end-of-course cramming and catch-up will compensate for missed activities. A particularly challenging burden for online instructors is to establish very clear expectations and ground rules with regard to regular participation. Of course, this applies to face-to-face settings as well; but the criticality of regular participation, especially to group activities in an online environment, is quite high since it is almost impossible to compensate at the end of an online course for such deficiencies.

Competency 18: Manage the instructional process through the appropriate use of technology.

(a) Use technology to support administrative functions.
(b) Use technology to seek and share information.
(c) Use technology to store and reuse instructional resources.
(d) Use technology to maintain the security and privacy of learner information.

Instructional processes (planning, preparing, facilitating, assessing, evaluating, and managing instruction) often involve technology. Broadly conceived, technology is the application of scientific and engineering knowledge to achieve a particular purpose. In the case of instructional management, the general purpose is to facilitate learning and improve human performance. Relevant sciences include cognitive science, learning theory, and organizational psychology. Related engineering disciplines include human factors, instructional design, and performance technology. Specific technologies that instructors use vary widely and may range from authoring tools and presentation systems to adaptive testing techniques and student management systems.

The instructor's primary function is not administrative in nature. However, because instructors have so much to do, it is imperative that they make effective use of technology to support administrative as well as other instructional requirements. Online resources for a variety of topics are now widely available. Online resources are critical to online learning environments and are increasingly included in face-to-face and blended learning environments. The reason for this is quite simply that online technologies make it both easy and cost-efficient to store, share, and reuse information and instructional resources (see Wiley, 2002). Because the implications of using technology have significant potential for improving learning, instructors are often required to manage the technology-based instructional resources associated with a course. However, there is an added burden for the online instructor who must exchange different kinds of information with the various participants in the learning process (e.g., learners, administrators, technicians, instructional designers, content experts, other instructors, etc.). An online instructor often needs to deal with a complex mechanism to ensure that the pre-course, course, and post-course tasks are both effective and efficient.

One consequence of technology-based learning environments is that information is sometimes too easily shared. With regard to copyright protected materials, this introduces a requirement for instructors in online learning environments to ensure that copyright restrictions are not violated (see Competency 3). Moreover, student grades and other confidential information are often stored in online systems; instructors, among others, are responsible for ensuring the security and privacy of this information. In sum, while technology introduces new possibilities, it also introduces new responsibilities.

CONCLUSION

Technology continues to change how instructors teach and how students learn. Moreover, knowledge of effective teaching and learning continues to grow. The International Board of Standards for Training, Performance and Instruction (ibstpi) has responded to these changes with the instructor competencies and associated performance statements discussed in this chapter. It should be obvious from this discussion that these competencies reflect growing emphasis on the integration of technology into teaching and learning and an increased appreciation for the varieties of effective instructional practice. Enhancing learning and facilitating performance is the mission of every instructor. Nevertheless, some particularities have to be considered according to the setting in which an instructor works. This chapter highlights these characteristics.

The Board has introduced the notion of competency clusters or domains in this extensive update of our instructor competencies: (1) professional foundations, (2) planning and preparation, (3) instructional methods and strategies, (4) assessment and evaluation, and (5) management. Each domain consists of several competencies that are intended to reflect best practice within that particular domain. In turn, each competency consists of a number of performance statements intended to reflect the skills, knowledge, and attitudes that contribute to instructor competence. However, performance statements are not intended to stand alone. The skills, knowledge, or attitudes described in a single performance statement are closely related to those found in other performance statements.

Every competent instructor is not expected to demonstrate every competency. In some settings instructors are not responsible for some of the competencies that comprise a particular domain. For example, in some training departments, instructors are not responsible for evaluation; in others, they are. The intention in these cases is to reflect what constitutes competence for whoever is responsible for such matters.

One notable change from the previous instructor standards identified by ibstpi is the grouping of a set of competencies in the domain of *Professional Foundations*. This domain reflects the notion that there is a foundational set of standards that every skilled instructor is expected to demonstrate. This foundation consists of: (1) communicating effectively, (2) updating and improving professional knowledge and skills, (3) complying with established ethical and legal standards, and (4) establishing and maintaining professional credibility. These competencies and their associated performance statements reflect the fundamental concept that an instructor is a professional practitioner with attendant expectations and responsibilities. Practitioners who completed our global survey rated the skills in the Professional Foundations domain as among the most important (see Chapter 6).

The two domains of *Planning and Preparation* and *Instructional Methods and Strategies* consist of what the professional community typically regard as the central knowledge, skills, and attitudes of competent instructors. These two domains contain many new and revised competencies that pertain explicitly to the integration of technology and to the diversity of teaching and learning situations. Some readers may be inclined to say that an instructor's professional life is growing more complicated on account of these changes. Others may say that these changes make being an instructor much more interesting as well as more challenging. The revised competencies in these two domains are consistent with both perspectives and are intended to help instructors better prepare themselves to succeed in the 21st century.

The two domains of *Assessment and Evaluation* and *Management* reflect many competencies that the professional community recognizes as performed by specialists, such as professional evaluators or training managers. Nonetheless, the knowledge, skills, and attitudes in these domains reflect the tight coupling of assessment, evaluation, and management issues to effective instruction. Moreover, the job title of those who perform specific assessment, evaluation, or management tasks is perhaps not as relevant as the skillful performance of the task to ensure the effectiveness of instruction. This has been ibstpi's primary concern in developing, validating, and publishing this updated set of instructor competencies.

NOTE

1.   The ibstpi instructor competencies and performance statements are copyrighted by the International Board of Standards for Training, Performance and Instruction (ibstpi). All rights reserved.

CHAPTER 5

USES OF THE IBSTPI
INSTRUCTOR COMPETENCIES

OVERVIEW

Thus far we have presented a context for instructor competencies, including a discussion of the evolution of instructor competence and an elaboration of how the ibstpi instructor competencies can be used in face-to-face, online, and blended settings. This chapter focuses on how the competencies might be used by individuals and organizations for a variety of purposes ranging from professional development to instructor certification.

The updated competencies represent more than the knowledge, skills, and attitudes expected of instructors in various settings. They provide an operational definition of an instructor that can be used by organizations to define job requirements and position descriptions, establish performance indicators, and improve professional development programs. These competencies also provide individuals with specific items that can be used to guide self-improvement.

The uses of the instructor competencies are explained below in terms of how they can improve instruction and enhance learning and performance. Uses by individuals and organizations are presented in separate sections followed by a section describing the role of these competencies in setting standards and forming the basis for instructor certification.

Instructor Competencies: Standards for Face-to-Face, Online, and Blended Settings, pages 59–70
Copyright © 2004 by Information Age Publishing
All rights of reproduction in any form reserved.   59

INDIVIDUAL USES

Individual instructors comprise the immediate and primary audience for these competencies. Other individuals will also find these competencies helpful in reflecting on and improving their work, including training managers, instructional designers, evaluators, human resources personnel, and academics. Table 5.1 presents the kinds of questions that individuals might reasonably expect to be addressed in these competencies.

Table 5.1.   Questions for Individual Use of Instructor Competencies

Individual User	*Representative Question*
Instructor	What can I do to improve my performance as an instructor?
Training manager	How might a meaningful and productive professional development program for instructors be developed?
Instructional designer	What instructor knowledge, skills, and attitudes are required to support a particular type of instruction?
Evaluator	How should individual instructor performance be evaluated?
Personnel manager	What characteristics should be used in hiring instructors?
Academic	What knowledge, skills, and attitudes should be developed in teacher preparation and train-the-trainer programs?

Instructors

A fundamental concern of all professional practitioners is to improve what they do. Instructors are quite naturally concerned with how they can become better instructors. For example, an instructor might address foundational knowledge and skills and reflect on his or her communication skills: "Am I using language that is appropriate for the audience, context, and culture?" Such a question might lead an instructor to reflect on the nature of the audience, context, and culture in order to become more aware of specific language that may or may not be appropriate in that situation. This concern is especially critical in a situation that is diverse and multicultural, as is increasingly common due to the globalization of training and education.

An instructor might focus on knowledge and skills in the area of planning and preparation and ask, "Have I planned and modified instruction to accommodate learners, settings, and presentation formats?" Some instructors are inclined to do whatever has been done previously without critically examining the appropriate use of instructional materials. Likewise, an instructor might focus on methods and strategies and ask, "Do I provide clear, timely, relevant, and specific feedback?" An instructor who embraces the notion of continuous self-improvement will seek answers to such questions. Asking such questions will improve instructor performance by helping to develop instructor competence as a reflective and professional practitioner.

Training Managers

Training managers serve an organization by being advocates for learning, development, and improved performance (Foxon et al., 2003). Part of this responsibility is the creation and support of an environment in which instructors continuously improve their knowledge and performance. In short, a training manager may be responsible for developing a professional development program for instructors. In order to do so, a training manager is required to understand what instructors do and which knowledge, skills, and attitudes are critical for success. Relevant questions to guide the development of a professional development program for instructors might be based on these competencies, such as: "How might instructors expand their knowledge of learning principles and instructional strategies?" or "How can instructors become better at recognizing the capabilities and limitations of media and technology?" Such questions can lead to the development of a series of professional development seminars or workshops and provide the foundation for identifying relevant topics and seminar leaders.

Instructional Designers

Among other things, instructional designers are responsible for developing instructional programs in response to existing or anticipated human performance problems (Richey et al., 2001). An essential instructional design skill is the ability to develop materials that support proposed instructional delivery methods and strategies. This often includes the preparation of instructor guides. An instructional designer must, therefore, be able to identify the specific instructor knowledge, skills, and attitudes required for successful implementation of a particular unit of instruction, module, or program. In short, instructional designers must understand what instructors do and specify what instructors should be doing to support a unit of instruction. Questions based on the ibstpi instructor competencies may help a designer in writing instructor guides. For example, an instructional designer might ask: "Which clarification and feedback strategies might help instructors with this unit of instruction?" or "What might instructors do in this unit of instruction to provide learners with opportunities to synthesize and integrate new knowledge?"

Evaluators

Evaluation is essential to improvement. In order to improve the performance of instructors, it is necessary to evaluate their performance. Indeed, the evaluation of instructional materials as well as instructors is cited as an instructional design competence (Richey et al., 2001). In order to effectively evaluate instructors, it is clear that one must understand what instructors do and why they do these things. The ibstpi instructor competencies provide a generic and widely applicable foundation for instructor evaluation. In the final section of this chapter, the use of these competencies in instructor certification will be discussed. For purposes of developing a systematic evaluation process for instructors, one could construct an instructor evaluation form based on Likert-type scale items constructed from relevant competencies and associated performance statements. One such item might be the following: "The instructor provided opportunities for reflection and review (1, strongly disagree; 2, disagree; 3, neutral; 4, agree; 5, strongly agree)." Learners are often asked to complete such evaluation forms at the conclusion of a course or program. Using the ibstpi instructor competencies as the basis for instructor evaluation, a training manager can then plan a meaningful professional development program constructed on the basis of recognized requirements and deficiencies.

Personnel Managers

Many organizations have personnel managers in human resource departments who are responsible for describing positions and then selecting and hiring appropriate people. In many training departments, a training manager is responsible for selecting and hiring instructors. Regardless, it is useful to consider many of these instructor competencies when describing instructor job requirements and selecting candidates to fill instructor positions. For example, an instructor job description might contain a statement such as this: "The person to be hired will be responsible for the planning, preparation, and delivery of instructional materials. Instructors must demonstrate effective presentation, facilitation, and questioning skills." Those responsible for selecting instructors might ask candidates to respond to such questions as: "In this unit of instruction, what might you do to encourage and support collaboration among learners?" or "Given the topic of this instructional unit and its location within a particular program of instruction, what might you do to establish relevance and increase learner motivation?"

Academics

Many universities have colleges or schools of education with teacher preparation programs. Some universities and corporations also have programs or courses aimed more specifically at the preparation of professional trainers. Academic personnel in these settings are responsible for developing meaningful sequences of courses and selecting appropriate content for specific courses. The ibstpi competencies can be used to guide curriculum development in such settings. For example, a university teacher preparation course or a corporate train-the-trainer course might be designed around the set of competencies and performance statements involving presentation, facilitation, and questioning skills.

ORGANIZATIONAL USES

Organizations involved in training and education comprise another primary audience for the ibstpi competencies. The general context for the organizational use of these instructor competencies is that of continuous improvement. Many organizational uses are already evident in the discussion of individual use in the previous section. The organizational units indicated in Table 5.2 are selected in order to suggest a range of potential use and are not necessarily separate and distinct. For example, train-the-trainer programs may be part of a training department, although many are offered by independent consultants. The point here is to indicate the kinds of organizational units that might find these competencies useful and to suggest particular uses for a variety of organizational users. Table 5.2 presents the kinds of questions that various organizations might reasonably expect to be addressed in these competencies. After exploring various organization uses of the competencies, the role of these competencies in instructor certification programs will be presented.

Training Departments

Training departments are often responsible for providing instructional services and support to other parts of an organization and to external clients. The performance of individual instructors is critical to the success of a training department. As indicated earlier, these competencies provide

Table 5.2. Questions for Organizational Use of Instructor Competencies

Organizational User	Representative Question
Training departments	How can the performance of instructors be improved to enhance overall department performance?
Personnel departments	What selection criteria are relevant for hiring instructors?
University programs	What knowledge, skills, and attitudes are relevant to include in a teacher preparation program?
Train-the-trainer programs	What topics are critically relevant for a train-the-trainer program?
Learning organization programs	Which knowledge, skills, and attitudes are required in order to implement a systematic, enterprise-wide learning organization effort?

sufficient detail to use in constructing instructor evaluation forms and evaluating instructors. They also provide a framework for establishing a professional development program for instructors. The ibstpi Board expects that many training departments will find these instructor competencies especially useful in combination with its competencies for training managers (Foxon et al., 2003) and instructional designers (Richey et al., 2001). Specific questions based on these competencies that might guide a continuous improvement effort within a training department are: "Are instructors making effective use of time management principles?" and "Are instructors aware of the ethical and legal implications of their practices?"

Personnel Departments

As mentioned earlier, these competencies can help guide the selection of qualified instructors. Many of the performance statements can be used during a job interview to determine if a candidate is a competent instructor. Additionally, a self-assessment survey can be constructed around selected performance statements to determine how a potential instructor thinks about his or her own behavior and capabilities. An example of such a self-assessment item is: "I routinely document my work as a foundation for future efforts (1, strongly disagree; 2, disagree; 3, neutral; 4, agree; 5, strongly agree)." Such a self-assessment survey might also be used to determine if potential instructors exhibit desirable attitudes toward their profession.

University Programs

Many universities have teacher preparation programs. In addition, train-the-trainer programs can be found in many government and defense organizations, in corporations and consulting companies, and in some universities. The curricula in such programs can be structured around the instructor competencies. Required courses might be based on the competencies in the Professional Foundations domain and in selected portions of other domains that are consistent with local practice. An example of such a course that might appear in a curriculum is "Effective Communication for Instructors." Such a course might have modules involving verbal and nonverbal language, cultural considerations in communication, active listening skills, and using technology to communicate.

Train-the-Trainer Programs

A principle use for these competencies is for the development of effective and efficient train-the-trainer programs. These programs are usually designed to fit local requirements and circumstances, which means that the set of relevant instructor competencies and performance statements are likely to be modified accordingly. Moreover, in developing a train-the-trainer curriculum around these competencies, an additional level of elaboration can be provided to match specific content, strategies, tools, and technologies in use in a particular setting or environment. For example, a train-the-trainer program might have a unit of instruction focused on stimulating and sustaining learning motivation and engagement within the context of a particular learning management system (LMS). This might involve training instructors on the use of the LMS to monitor individual learner participation and to provide private and individualized feedback to learners.

Learning Organization Programs

Organizations have long sought means and mechanisms to support continuous improvement. In the modern, global, information-age economy, it is commonly accepted that organizations must become flexible, agile, knowledge-driven units in order to enjoy continued success (Senge, 1990). The realization of a genuine organizational learning environment involves many human-dependent variables that can be affected in a positive way by instruction (Morecroft & Sterman, 1994). In short, a commitment to becoming a learning organization often involves a commitment to developing knowledge management systems and instructional systems that are integrated with everyday performance support systems (Spector & Edmonds, 2002; Spector & Wang, 2002). Questions based on these competencies that are likely to prove beneficial in achieving an effective learning organization include the following: "Is technology used to seek and share information throughout the organization at all levels?" and "Is technology used to store and reuse instructional resources on a regular basis throughout all units of the organization?"

Additionally, a genuine learning organization makes effective use of on-the-job training (OJT), reminiscent of the earlier description of apprenticeship (see Chapter 1). In too many cases, there is no special training or preparation provided for key personnel who become responsible for OJT. The ibstpi instructor competencies can be used to ensure that critical OJT efforts are effective and efficient. For example, key personnel who become responsible for training newcomers might be selected based on their aptitude for instruction as determined by the instructor self-assessment instrument described earlier. Training for key OJT personnel can be designed around specific performance statements such as: "Demonstrate how to apply knowledge and skills in realistic settings" and "Provide opportunities for newcomers to practice recently acquired skills in non-threatening situations."

INSTRUCTOR COMPETENCIES AND CERTIFICATION

The instructor competencies published by ibstpi in 1993 (see Appendix A) became the basis for an internationally accepted certification for technical trainers. The Board is quite proud that the 1993 competencies came to be recognized as the standard for technical trainers all over the world and enjoyed 10 years of international prominence with more than 15,000 certification tests administered. As indicated at the beginning of this chapter, the development, validation and implementation of international standards to advance training, instruction, learning and performance improvement for individuals and organizations is the Board's primary mission. However, 10 years is a relatively long period of time for any set of standards to remain in such widespread use. Moreover, there have been so many changes in instructional practice and technology since 1993 that ibstpi decided that it was time to replace those standards with an up-to-date set of instructor competencies (see Chapter 1). The process involved in this effort has been described (see Chapter 2) and the validation of the final set of instructor competencies is described in the next chapter. What follows is a discussion of the nature of instructor standards and their use as the basis for industry-wide certification programs.

STANDARDS

The concept of a standard involves something (an activity or an object) that is established and recognized as having a desirable level of excellence or quality against which specific items might be compared in order to determine their adequacy. Key aspects of this definition include: (a) an established basis for the standards, (b) public recognition of the standards, and (c) a level of specificity that supports comparative assessments. The ibstpi standards consist of sets of competency statements organized in domains with a number of specific performance statements associated with each competency statement. These standards have been established through a long, rigorous, empirically based process (see Chapters 2 and 6). The competency development process for this set of standards required more than four years of effort and is grounded in the empirical evidence of more than 1,300 professional instructors worldwide as well as an extensive review of the relevant literature and many instructor interviews and focus group discussions. We are confident that this set of instructor standards reflects the current best practices of instructors.

Because the 1993 ibstpi Instructor Competencies received such international prominence and became the internationally recognized standard for technical trainers in such a short period of time, we are also confident that this improved and up-to-date set of standards will likewise receive similar public recognition and prominence. Finally, as was the case with the previous standards, this updated set of standards is sufficiently specific to support comparative assessments. As indicated throughout Chapter 4, specific performance statements lend themselves to interpretation in face-to-face, online, and blended settings. This attribute makes this set of competencies even more worthwhile for certifying instructors in a variety of settings.

While the 1993 standards were quite robust and useful, they were limited to face-to-face settings. Since 1993, online learning has expanded technologically as well as geographically. As noted previously, the Board was prompted by industry to consider the development of standards for online instructors and that process led us to develop a set of competencies that could be used in a variety of settings and locations. We believe that it is particularly worthwhile to think of all instructional settings as potentially blended due to the rapid and widespread changes in technologies, strategies, learning communities, and so on. This set of standards is consistent with the notion of blended settings while being useful in face-to-face and online settings.

CERTIFICATION

The process of certification in the context of a profession or industry involves the measurement and reporting of the competence of individual practitioners (Gilley, Geis, & Seyfer, 1987). A certification process thus requires the existence of standards that represent competencies for a profession or industry. In order to be measurable, these competencies must be further elaborated; in the case of the ibstpi standards, this elaboration takes the form of performance statements associated with each competency; these performance statements reflect how an individual may exhibit the relevant competency.

Once standards are established and recognized, how might certification be accomplished? With regard to instructors and consistent with the ibstpi definition of a competency, there are related sets of knowledge, skills, and attitudes associated with competence. This implies that a knowledge test by itself is not sufficient to establish instructor competence since it must also be established that an individual can perform particular instructional tasks and activities satisfactorily. At a minimum, the certification process should establish that the individual has adequate knowledge, can perform particular tasks, and has the relevant attitudes desirable of a competent instructor.

Components of a Certification Examination

There are two primary components of a certification examination for instructors: a knowledge test and a performance demonstration. A test can be used to establish whether or not an individual has the relevant knowledge. The knowledge test can consist of a variety of short-answer items as well as problem scenarios to which the individual is asked to respond. Some indication of the existence of desirable instructor attitudes might also be gathered from particular test items.

Individuals must also demonstrate their competence to an unbiased certifying body or agency. The demonstration of instructor competence might consist of videotaping one or more sample sessions with learners and having the certifying agency assess whether or not the instructor has the relevant skills. As with a knowledge test, a videotape of an instructional session might also reveal whether or not an individual has attitudes desired in competent instructors. Competence in an online environment may be reflected in an instructor portfolio that captures instructor–learner dialogues associated with presentations and other learner activities from a learning management system. It should be obvious that the assessment of attitudes is difficult and more complicated than the assessment of relevant knowledge and skills, which have historically been the focus of competency-based certifications.

The certification process associated with the 1993 ibstpi instructor competencies involved both a knowledge test and a performance component. The latter consisted of videotaped submissions of sample sessions. Due to the wider variety of instructional settings covered in this set of instructor competencies, it no longer makes sense to restrict the performance demonstration to videotaped sessions. Some instructors teach in online and blended settings that make videotaping impossible or inappropriate. The process of training raters for video-based assessments is also costly and introduces significant expenses and delays into the process of certification.

The ibstpi Board is convinced that a performance component is an essential aspect of a certification examination. However, there are other means of demonstrating performance, including the creation of instructor portfolios. These portfolios can be tailored to particular instructional settings. Specific requirements for an instructor portfolio should be established by an independent certifying agency just as the items to be included in the knowledge examination should be established, administered, and scored by an independent agency.

The Certification Process

Different industries and professions may develop modified subsets of the ibstpi competencies to satisfy the best practices in that industry. For example, in some corporate settings, instructors are not responsible for or expected to demonstrate competence in assessing learning or evaluating instructional effectiveness. As stated earlier in this volume, not every instructor is expected to exhibit every competency. Moreover, it is expected that organizations will adapt these competencies to fit local practice. However, when an industry or profession decides to go forward with instructor certification, it is quite likely that most of these instructor competencies will in some way be relevant to the certification process. The Board expects that all of the competencies in the Professional Foundations domain will be relevant to certification. Most of the competencies in the Planning and Preparation and in Methods and Strategies domains are likely to be relevant to certification as these represent what most instructors do on a recurring basis. Many of the competencies and performance statements in the Assessment and Evaluation and in Management domains are likely to prove relevant to certification as well. In any case, what is critical for a certification process is that an independent certification agency be established and recognized within the profession or industry. Without such a recognized independent agency, a certification process is subject to bias and manipulation.

CONCLUSION

In this chapter we have described how individuals and organizations can make use of the ibstpi instructor competencies. We have also indicated how they constitute the basis for instructor standards and can provide the basis for industry-wide certification programs. The ibstpi Board is committed to advancing professional practice with regard to training, instruction, and performance improvement. When instructors do well, the benefits are widespread. These competencies can be used to improve what instructors do and thereby help organizations become genuine learning organizations that can thrive in a changing world.

CHAPTER 6

THE COMPETENCY VALIDATION STUDY

OVERVIEW

The previous chapters have focused on the competencies for instructors in face-to-face, online, and blended settings and on how they might be used by individuals and organizations. In this chapter, we examine how the competencies are supported by evidence from research. The International Board of Standards for Training, Performance and Instruction employs a rigorous empirical approach to identify and validate competencies (see Chapter 2 for a discussion of the ibstpi competency development model). Below, we discuss the sources that provide a foundation for the competencies and the results of a validation study that offers empirical evidence regarding the usefulness, criticality, and appropriateness of the competencies for instructors in various settings.

FOUNDATION OF THE IBSTPI INSTRUCTOR COMPETENCIES

1993 Instructor Competencies

The instructor standards published by ibstpi in 1993 included 14 competencies with 83 corresponding performance statements (see Appendix A). These served as a foundation for the updated competences and perfor-

Instructor Competencies: Standards for Face-to-Face, Online, and Blended Settings, pages 71–87
Copyright © 2004 by Information Age Publishing
All rights of reproduction in any form reserved.

mance statements described in this book. The 1993 competencies focused on instruction as it relates to preparation, delivery, evaluation, and follow-up in face-to-face settings. At the time of their development, the statements were identified based on the Board's understanding of the decisions, actions, and behaviors that competent instructors must demonstrate. While current knowledge about learning and technology has advanced in recent years, some fundamental tenets of instruction have not changed. These views are reflected in the updated competencies.

Table 6.1 shows how the current ibstpi instructor competencies have been updated from the 1993 set. Six competency statements that were not in the 1993 list are now in the updated standards. Another six statements from the 1993 set were expanded to reflect the changing roles of instructors and the use of technology for teaching and learning. Four other competencies were worded differently to update terminology and two competencies in the updated list were stated exactly as they were in 1993. Furthermore, the 1993 competency—*use instructional methods appropriately*—has been elevated to the domain called Instructional Methods and Strategies. This domain includes eight competencies related to the use of instructional methods to promote learning and performance.

Table 6.1. Comparison of Updated Instructor Competencies to 1993 Statements

Updated competencies	1993 competencies	Changes to competencies
Communicate effectively.	Demonstrate effective communication skills.	Minor change
Update and improve one's professional knowledge and skills.	—	New competency
Comply with established ethical and legal standards.	—	New competency
Establish and maintain professional credibility.	Establish and maintain instructor credibility.	No change
Plan instructional methods and materials.	Analyze course materials and learner information.	Expanded concept
Prepare for instruction.	Ensure preparation of the instructional site.	Expanded concept
Stimulate and sustain learner motivation and engagement.	Provide positive reinforcements and motivational incentives.	Expanded concept
Demonstrate effective presentation skills.	Demonstrate effective presentation skills.	No change
Demonstrate effective facilitation skills.	—	New competency

Table 6.1.   Comparison of Updated Instructor Competencies to 1993 Statements (Cont.)

Updated competencies	1993 competencies	Changes to competencies
Demonstrate effective questioning skills.	Demonstrate effective questioning skills and technique.	Minor change
Provide clarification and feedback.	Respond appropriately to learners' needs for clarification or feedback.	Minor change
Promote retention of knowledge and skills.	—	New competency
Promote transfer of knowledge and skills.	—	New competency
Use media and technology to enhance learning and performance.	Use media effectively.	Expanded concept
Assess learning and performance.	Evaluate learner performance.	Minor change
Evaluate instructional effectiveness.	Evaluate delivery of instruction. Report evaluation information.	Expanded concept
Manage an environment that fosters learning and performance.	Manage the learning environment.	Expanded concept
Manage the instructional process through the appropriate use of technology.	—	New competency
—	Use instructional methods appropriately.	Elevated to the domain level

The Influence of Theory, Research, and Practice

In addition to previous competencies developed by ibstpi, the updated instructor standards were influenced by theory, research, and practice related to teaching and learning. Over 200 theoretical, conceptual, and empirical studies found in books, journal articles, and conference proceedings were examined to provide a foundation for the updated competencies (see Chapter 4 as well as Ganesan, 2004; Spector & de la Teja, 2001).

Furthermore, materials from several train-the-trainer courses used in corporate and educational settings were reviewed to examine current practice. Instructor and leader guides as well as participant materials were obtained and reviewed from the following areas: banking, financial services, a for-profit online university, manufacturing, and pharmaceuticals.

The ibstpi Board cohosted a meeting of experts in the distance education field (see Goodyear et al., 2001) and served as an expert panel to identify instructor competencies. Members of ibstpi also conducted six focus groups with individuals from business, academia, and professional organizations to obtain further input on the competencies and performance statements identified by the Board.

WORLDWIDE VALIDATION STUDY

Purpose and Scope

A worldwide validation study was conducted to gather empirical evidence about an initial set of 21 competencies and 134 performance statements approved by ibstpi. The purpose of the study was to determine the level of criticality of the competencies and performance statements in the initial list for instructors in face-to-face and online settings and to gather comments on each. The purpose of the open-ended comments was to help refine the language to reflect an international audience in diverse settings, and ensure that no critical area of work had been overlooked.

By asking respondents with experience in either face-to-face or online instruction to rate the criticality of the competencies for that setting, we were able to test the assumption drawn by the Board that there was a basic set of competencies for instructors that did not differ by instructional setting. Therefore, we believed that differences in perceived criticality between face-to-face and online instructor competencies would be minimal.

Procedures

A validation instrument was developed and made available via the Internet and on paper. Respondents were recruited and data were collected over a 3-month period. Data were summarized by face-to-face and online setting and were used by ibstpi to develop a final list of competencies and performance statements.

Instrumentation

The validation instrument was created, pilot tested, and refined. The pilot instrument included demographic questions and criticality statements. Twenty-seven responses were collected. One duplicate performance statement was deleted and one typographical error was fixed during pilot testing. The original design of the instrument required 174 responses. This length was found to be problematic for many online respondents. To address this problem, the instrument was clustered into four separate parts so that the respondents would submit the survey when each part was completed. The final instrument consisted of a section with respondent background characteristics and three competency sections, along with a scale to indicate the criticality of specific statements and to enter additional comments about the statements or the survey as a whole. While the primary means for distribution of the survey was in a Web-based form, a paper-based version was also available. By far, most responses came via the Internet—the ratio was about 35 Internet responses for every paper-based response.

Section 1: Respondent Background Characteristics

Eighteen demographic questions were asked to collect extensive background data on the respondents to establish a rationale for the level of generalizability of data. We sought data on the respondents in three general areas:

- *Personal profile*, including gender, age, educational background, and field of expertise.
- *Experiential profile*, including number of years of experience in face-to-face, blended, and online settings; perceived level of instructor and technology expertise; experience as an online student; frequency of computer use; and experience developing a Web page.
- *Job profile*, including geographic location of job, type of organizational setting, focus of the job, percentage of time devoted to instruction or training, and major language used on the job.

Section 2: Criticality Statements

Respondents were asked to rate the level of criticality of the 21 competencies and 134 performance statements for instructors in face-to-face and online settings. Competency statements were listed in italics while the performance statements were written in a standard font. A scale of 1 to 5 was used, with 5 being very highly critical to their job and 1 having no criticality to their job. Individuals were asked to rate the criticality of statements in a particular setting *only* if they had teaching experience in that setting. A section for comments was included after each group of competencies and related performance statements in the paper-based version and after each statement in the online version. Figure 6.1 shows the validation survey items for statements related to the competency of questioning.

Section 3: Additional Comments

Four open-ended questions were asked regarding any additional skills, suggestions for rewording, comments comparing online versus classroom teaching, and any general comments.

Circle how important each statement is in relation to *your job* by using the following scale:
1 = None, 2 = Low, 3 = Moderate, 4 = High, 5 = Very High

	Classroom Criticality	Online Criticality
81. Demonstrate effective questioning skills.	1 2 3 4 5	1 2 3 4 5
82. Ask questions linked to goals and objectives.	1 2 3 4 5	1 2 3 4 5
83. Use questions to promote learn and motivation.	1 2 3 4 5	1 2 3 4 5
84. Ensure clarity, relevance, and specificity of questions.	1 2 3 4 5	1 2 3 4 5
85. Follow up on questions from learners.	1 2 3 4 5	1 2 3 4 5
86. Use a variety of question types and levels.	1 2 3 4 5	1 2 3 4 5
87. Direct and redirect questions that promote learning.	1 2 3 4 5	1 2 3 4 5
88. Use questions to generate and guide discussions.	1 2 3 4 5	1 2 3 4 5
89. Build on responses to previous questions in subsequent learning activities.	1 2 3 4 5	1 2 3 4 5

Figure 6.1.   Validation survey items for statements related to questioning.

Sample Selection

Following approved Syracuse University Human Subjects Institutional Review Board procedures, the ibstpi Board sent requests for participation in the validation study to training institutions, professional organizations, professional electronic mailing lists, conference participants, and other worldwide contacts in training, teaching, and distance education. These sources were identified through extensive Internet searches and Board member contacts. Trainers and instructors were contacted via email, phone, and newsletter announcements. The URL containing the Informed Consent form and a link to the validation instrument and the address to acquire a paper-based version were provided in each communiqué. The paper-based version of the survey was mailed to any individual who requested it. In addition, a link to the instrument was included on the ibstpi.org website. The instrument, therefore, was available to anyone visiting the site on his or her own accord. Since the sample was not selected on a random basis, the profile data cannot be assumed to be representative of the entire population of instructors or trainers. The intent was to solicit responses from experienced instructors and trainers worldwide.

Demographics of the Respondents

A large, diverse sample (N = 1327) responded to the request to participate in the validation study. Not every respondent, however, answered
every question. Percentages represent the proportion of those who
responded to each individual question. These are summarized by the three
profiles of personal, experiential, and occupational.

Respondent Personal Profile

Table 6.2 provides data about the gender, age, and educational background of respondents who completed the validation survey. A slightly
higher percentage (55.3%) of respondents were male (613 of 1109) while
44.7% percent were female (496 of 1109). The average age of respondents
was 41.1 years old, ranging from age 20 to 70. The majority was between 30
and 49 years old. Many respondents had either a master's degree (24.5%,
271 of 1107) or an undergraduate degree (22.6%; 250 of 1107).

Table 6.2. Personal Profiles of Respondents to Validation Survey

Characteristic	N	Percentage
Gender		
Female	496	44.7
Male	613	55.3
Total Number of Respondents	1,109	100.0
Age		
20–29	170	15.9
30–39	343	32.2
40–49	293	27.5
50–59	215	20.2
60–69	43	4.0
70–79	2	0.2
Total Number of Respondents	1,066	100.0
Educational Background		
Secondary	42	3.8
Vocational/Certificate	83	7.5
Associate Degree	66	6.0
Undergraduate Degree	250	22.6
Graduate Diploma	112	10.1
Master's Degree	271	24.5
Post Master's Degree	88	7.9
Doctorate	164	14.8
Other	31	2.8
Total Number of Respondents	1,107	100.0

Table 6.3 reveals that respondents came from diverse fields of expertise. The majority considered themselves experts in training and development (57%, 625 of 1097), adult education (47.3%, 519 of 1097), or education (39.1%, 429 of 1097).

Table 6.3.   Field of Expertise for Survey Respondents

Field of Expertise*	N	Percentage
Training and Development	625	57.0
Adult Education	519	47.3
Education	429	39.1
Instructional Design	356	32.5
Computer Science	345	31.4
Instructional Technology	314	28.6
Information Systems	313	28.5
Online Learning	222	20.2
Business	216	19.7
Management and Administration	203	18.5
Organizational Development	163	14.9
Communications	159	14.5
Science and Engineering	131	11.9
Human Resources	126	11.5
Psychology & Medicine	122	11.2
Other	91	8.3

* Respondents selected multiple fields of expertise so total is greater than 100%. N = 1097.

Respondent Experiential Profile

Table 6.4 shows that almost all of the respondents had experience as an instructor or trainer in face-to-face settings (98.8%, 1089 of 1102, M = 10.9 years). Less than half of the respondents had experience teaching in online (40.9%, 452 of 1105, M = 3.5 years) or blended settings (39.8%, 433 of 1087, M = 3.2 years). Because there were high numbers of respondents with online and blended experience, we were able to compare their responses credibly with those having only face-to-face experience.

A large percentage of respondents (87.9%) rated their expertise as an instructor or trainer as either high or very high (975 of 1110). Expertise with technology to support learning was also rated high or very high (74.5%, 826 of 1109). Three-fourths (75.1%) of the respondents (832 of 1108) had created a Web page and 68.9% (759 of 1101) had experience as

**Table 6.4.   Experiential Profile for Respondents
to Validation Survey**

Characteristic	N	Percentage
Experience in Face-to-Face Settings		
Yes	1089	98.8
No	13	1.2
Total Number of Respondents	1102	100.0
Number of Years		
0–10	636	60.6
11–20	279	26.6
21 +	134	12.8
Total Number of Respondents	1049	100.0
Experience in Online Settings		
Yes	452	40.9
No	653	59.1
Total Number of Respondents	1105	100.0
Number of Years		
0–5	372	84.0
6–10	55	12.4
10 +	16	3.6
Total Number of Respondents	443	100.0
Experience in Blended Settings		
Yes	433	39.8
No	654	60.2
Total Number of Respondents	1087	100.0
Number of Years		
0–5	370	86.9
6–10	48	11.2
10 +	8	1.9
Total Number of Respondents	426	100.0
Perceived Level of Instructor Expertise		
None	2	0.2
Low	9	0.8
Moderate	124	11.2
High	549	49.5
Very High	426	38.4
Total Number of Respondents	1110	100.0

**Table 6.4.   Experiential Profile for Respondents
to Validation Survey (Cont.)**

Characteristic	N	Percentage
Perceived Level of Expertise Using Technology in Instruction		
None	8	0.7
Low	51	4.6
Moderate	224	20.2
High	470	42.4
Very High	356	32.1
Total Number of Respondents	1109	100.0
Experience as a Student in an Online Course		
Yes	759	68.9
No	342	31.1
Total Number of Respondents	1101	100.0
Frequency of Use of Computers		
Never	27	2.4
Seldom	93	8.4
Occasionally	183	16.5
Often	275	24.8
Very Often	531	47.9
Total Number of Respondents	1109	100.0
Experience with Web Page Development		
Yes	832	75.1
No	276	24.9
Total Number of Respondents	1108	100.0

a student in an online course. Finally, 72.7% (806 of 1109) use the computer and information technologies often or very often.

Respondent Job Profile

Table 6.5 reveals that most respondents (73%; 808 of 1107) listed instructor or trainer as their job focus. Others noted classroom teacher as their focus (37.4%; 414 of 1107). Design, development, facilitation, and management were each listed by at least one-fourth of the respondents. In addition, many respondents (58.1%; 633 of 1089) devote at least half of their time on the job to instruction or training.

Many respondents work in educational settings (60.7%; 677 of 1115), followed by high-tech organizations (23%; 257 of 1115). The remaining types of organizations were each represented by less than 10% of the respondents (see Table 6.6). Furthermore, most respondents were from the United States or Canada (75.5%; 836 of 1107), followed by Western

Table 6.5.   Job Focus of Respondents

Job Focus*	N	Percentage
Instructor/Trainer	808	73.0
Classroom Teacher	414	37.4
Designer	327	29.5
Developer	321	29.0
Facilitator	288	26.0
Management	286	25.8
Distance Educator	158	14.3
Tutors	94	8.5
Moderator	59	5.3
Other	84	7.6

* Respondents selected multiple jobs so total is greater than 100%. N = 1007.

Europe (9.8%; 108 of 1107) (see Table 6.7). This was counterbalanced by international representation on the ibstpi Board when data from the validation study were analyzed and the competencies and performance statements were refined.

Table 6.6.   Organizational Setting of Respondents

Type of Organizational Setting	N	Percentage*
Educational Institutions	677	60.7
High-Tech Organizations	257	23.0
Government	86	7.7
Software Development	81	7.3
Manufacturing	79	7.1
Telecommunications	69	6.2
Nongovernmental	64	5.7
Association/Nonprofits	62	5.6
Financial Services	57	5.1
Health Care	55	4.9
Military	45	4.0
Retail	29	2.6
Utilities	29	2.6
Transportation	25	2.2
Pharmaceuticals	25	2.2
Intergovernmental	14	1.3
Other	129	11.6

* Respondents selected multiple settings so total is greater than 100%.

Table 6.7.   Geographic Location Respondents

Geographic Location	N	Percentage
U.S. & Canada	836	75.5
Western Europe	108	9.8
Asia	70	6.3
Australia and New Zealand	39	3.5
Latin America and Mexico	30	2.7
Middle East and Northern Africa	23	2.1
Pacific Region	21	1.9
Eastern Europe	16	1.4
Caribbean	16	1.4
Sub-Saharan Africa	11	1.0
Other	13	1.2

Findings of the Validation Study

Data obtained from the individuals who participated in the validation study were used to establish the usefulness and appropriateness of the competencies for instructors in face-to-face and online settings. Open-ended comments made by the respondents were also used to revise statements for meaning and clarity. Using the criticality data and the open-ended comments, ibstpi analyzed, debated, and acted upon each statement in one of three ways: (1) retain as stated, (2) revise, or (3) delete.

Using this process, the initial set of 21 competencies and 134 performance statements was refined to include 18 competencies supported by 98 performance statements. Table 6.8 shows the comparison between the initial competencies and improvements made as a result of the validation study.

Support for the Instructor Competencies

Table 6.9 provides the average criticality ratings for the competencies. In nearly all cases, the final list of competencies included statements that received a rating of 4.0 or above on a 5-point scale for both face-to-face and online settings.

The competencies in the Professional Foundations domain were among the most highly rated of all statements; all four were retained in the final list of competencies. In the Planning and Preparation domain, one competency remained unchanged, one was reworded for clarity, and one was deleted. These decisions were based on open-ended comments made by respondents and the Board's belief that the initial statements provided support for other competencies.

Table 6.8.   Summary of Revisions to Competencies and Performance Statements

Initial Competency	# of Initial Performance Statements	Final Competency	# of Final Performance Statements
Communicate effectively.	7	Retained	5
Update and improve one's professional knowledge and skills.	8	Retained	5
Establish and maintain professional credibility.	6	Retained	5
Comply with established ethical and legal standards.	7	Retained	6
Prepare for instruction.	7	Retained	6
Adapt instructional methods and materials.	5	Revised to—Plan instructional methods and materials.	6
Organize the learning environment.	4	Deleted	0
Recognize and accommodate learner diversity.*	3	Deleted, included in performance statements	0
Stimulate learner motivation and engagement.	8	Revised to—Stimulate and sustain learner motivation and engagement.	6
Demonstrate effective presentation skills.	5	Retained	5
Demonstrate effective facilitation skills.	9	Retained	6
Demonstrate effective questioning skills.	8	Retained	6
Provide clarification and feedback.	9	Retained	6
Promote retention of knowledge and skills.	5	Retained	5
Promote transfer of knowledge and skills.	7	Retained	6
Use media and technology to enhance learning and performance.*	7	Retained	5
Assess learning and performance.	8	Retained	5
Evaluate instructional effectiveness.	4	Retained	5
Document and report evaluation data.*	3	Deleted, included in performance statement	0
Manage the learning environment.	9	Revised to—Manage a learning environment that fosters learning and performance.	6
Use technology to manage information, learning, and performance.*	5	Revised to—Manage the instructional process through appropriate use of technology.	4

* Competency statement rated less than 4.0

Table 6.9. Criticality of Competencies in Face-to-Face and Online Settings

Competency Statement	Face-to-Face Setting				Online Setting			
	Average Rating	SD	N	Rank	Average Rating	SD	N	Rank
Communicate effectively.	4.71	0.58	822	1	4.64	0.72	330	1
Update and improve one's professional knowledge and skills.	4.49	0.74	803	3/4	4.59	0.65	320	2
Establish and maintain professional credibility.	4.36	0.86	797	8	4.32	0.89	314	11
Comply with established ethical and legal standards.	4.45	0.81	787	5	4.51	0.77	314	6
Prepare for instruction.	4.61	0.64	787	2	4.57	0.75	313	3
Adapt instructional methods and materials.	4.16	0.82	778	15	4.24	0.88	307	16
Organize the learning environment.	4.12	0.85	775	16/17	4.28	0.95	302	13
Recognize and accommodate learner diversity.	3.96	0.91	616	18/19	3.92	0.94	237	21
Stimulate learner motivation and engagement.	4.38	0.72	602	7	4.38	0.81	231	8/9
Demonstrate effective presentation skills.	4.49	0.70	600	3/4	4.02	1.01	229	20
Demonstrate effective facilitation skills.	4.23	0.84	583	13	4.19	1.04	220	17
Demonstrate effective questioning skills.	4.28	0.77	586	11	4.25	0.89	224	15
Provide clarification and feedback.	4.43	0.67	582	6	4.52	0.74	221	5
Promote retention of knowledge and skills.	4.35	0.77	577	9	4.37	0.83	214	10
Promote transfer of knowledge and skills.	4.30	0.82	571	10	4.38	0.81	214	8/9
Use media and technology to enhance learning and performance.	3.96	0.95	574	18/19	4.54	0.68	213	4
Assess learning and performance.	4.12	0.94	555	16/17	4.27	0.87	205	14
Evaluate instructional effectiveness.	4.25	0.85	548	12	4.29	0.88	204	12
Document and report evaluation data.	3.93	1.05	540	20	4.04	1.03	200	19
Manage the learning environment.	4.19	0.87	535	14	4.16	1.00	197	18
Use technology to manage information, learning and performance.	3.76	1.02	539	21	4.46	0.79	200	7

In the Instructional Methods and Strategies domain, one competency—*Recognize and accommodate learner diversity*—was deleted. This statement was the only one rated below 4.0 by instructors with experience in both face-to-face and online settings. Even though it was deleted, the Board decided the concept was very important and retained it within performance statements (see, e.g., *Determine relevant characteristics of learners, other participants, and instructional settings* and *Plan or modify instruction to accommodate learners, instructional settings, and presentation formats*). Another competency in this domain, *Use media and technology to enhance learning and performance*, was retained despite a lower rating for face-to-face settings (3.96). The rating for online settings was high (4.54) and the Board concluded this competency was critical for all instructors, especially when future vision is considered.

Turning to the Assessment and Evaluation domain, two of the three competencies were retained. The third competency, *Document and report evaluation data*, was rated at 3.93 for face-to-face settings and 4.04 for online settings. The three supporting statements for this competency were also rated below 4.0 for both face-to-face and online settings. Furthermore, open-ended comments suggested that many instructors who completed the validation survey are not responsible for these tasks. While the competency was deleted, the Board felt the idea was important and decided to include it as a performance statement to support the competency *Evaluate instructional effectiveness*.

Both competencies in the Management domain were revised for clarity and meaning. One was reworded to link the concept of management to learning and performance in instructional settings. The other competency, *Use technology to manage information, learning, and performance*, was reworded to *Manage the instructional process through the appropriate use of technology.* The ibstpi Board defines technology broadly and changed the emphasis in this competency by moving management to the first part of the statement.

Support for Performance Statements

Rankings for the supporting performance statements were also examined for criticality ratings less then 4.0. Table 6.10 shows the number of performance statements rated between 3.99 and 3.75 and between 3.74 and 3.50 for each competency statement. For face-to-face settings, 25 statements were rated between 3.75 and 3.99 and 22 were rated between 3.50 and 3.74. For online settings, 25 performance statements were rated between 3.75 and 3.99 and six were rated less than 3.75. Only one statement, *Document one's work as a foundation for future efforts, publications, or professional presentations,* was rated below 3.50. Based on these data and comments from the respondents, the final number of performance statements included to support the instructor competencies was reduced from 134 to 98.

Table 6.10. Performance Statement Ratings

Competency Statement	Number of performance statements	Face to Face Setting		Online Setting	
		Number of statements with ratings between 3.99–3.75	Number of statements with ratings under 3.75	Number of statements with ratings between 3.99–3.75	Number of statements with ratings under 3.75
Communicate effectively.	7	1	1	2	1
Update and improve one's professional knowledge and skills.	8	2	4	2	1
Establish and maintain professional credibility.	6	0	0	0	0
Comply with established and ethical legal standards.	7	0	0	0	0
Prepare for instruction.	7	2	1	1	0
Adapt instructional methods and materials.	5	0	1	0	0
Organize the learning environment.	4	2	1	1	0
Recognize and accommodate learner diversity.	3	2	0	2	0
Stimulate learner motivation and engagement.	8	1	0	0	0
Demonstrate effective presentation skills.	5	0	0	2	0
Demonstrate effective facilitation skills.	9	2	0	3	0
Demonstrate effective questioning skills	8	0	0	1	0
Provide clarification and feedback.	9	2	0	1	0
Promote retention of knowledge and skills.	5	1	0	0	0
Promote transfer of knowledge and skills.	7	1	3	4	1
Use media and technology to enhance learning and performance.	7	2	3	0	0
Assess learning and performance.	8	3	3	4	1
Evaluate instructional effectiveness.	4	1	0	0	0
Document and report evaluation data.	3	0	3	1	2
Manage the learning environment.	9	1	0	1	0
Use technology to manage information, learning and performance.	5	2	2	0	0

CONCLUSION

The results of this study provide empirical evidence that the instructor competencies identified and validated by ibstpi apply to a wide range of settings. The competency *Communicate effectively* was ranked the highest by respondents with experience in both face-to-face and online settings (4.71 and 4.64, respectively). The most compelling evidence to support our conclusion comes from comparing the difference between means, and the ranking of the criticality ratings by setting. In the first case, 15 of the initial 21 competencies were within 0 to 0.1 points. Three were within 0.11 to 0.16 points. Of those, two were deleted from the final list, and for the third, both ratings were above 4.0.

A few differences were observed between face-to-face and online instructors. For example, the lowest-ranked competency for the face-to-face setting was *Use technology to manage information, learning, and performance.* This statement was rated 0.70 points higher for the online setting. In addition, the competency *Use media and technology to enhance learning and performance* was rated 0.58 points higher for the online setting. These results suggest differences in the way instructors in face-to-face and online settings perceive the integral nature of technology and the specifics about how it is used differently depending on setting.

One other difference is worth noting. The criticality rating for the statement *Demonstrate effective presentation skills* was 0.47 points higher for the face-to-face setting. While both groups rated it above 4.0, this is another example of the difference in execution of the skills by setting, however retaining the importance generally for both settings. Despite these few differences, ibstpi maintains the position that a core set of competencies exists for instructors in all settings.

EPILOGUE

The mission of the International Board of Standards for Training, Performance and Instruction (ibstpi) is to develop, validate, and promote implementation of international standards to advance training, instruction, learning, and performance improvement for individuals and organizations. Our basic intent is to improve individual and organizational learning and performance and, in doing so, to promote the quality and integrity of professional practice.

Consistent with our mission, the updated competencies for instructors reflect our continuing commitment to improve professional practice. They provide one of the most comprehensive lists of instructor competencies in existence. Nonetheless, there is no way to provide an exhaustive set of instructor competencies due to the rich variety of instructional situations and circumstances. Consequently, we expect that individuals and organizations will adapt and customize these competencies appropriately for local practice and culture.

We are hopeful that the instructor competencies offered in this book advance learning and performance improvement for individuals and organizations throughout the world.

Instructor Competencies: Standards for Face-to-Face, Online, and Blended Settings, page 89
Copyright © 2004 by Information Age Publishing
All rights of reproduction in any form reserved.

REFERENCES

American Society for Training and Development. *ASTD Learning Circuits Glossary.* Retrieved June 11, 2004, from http://www.learningcircuits.org/glossary.html

Anderson, B. V., & Gipe, J. P. (1983). Creativity as a mediating variable in inferential reading comprehension. *Reading Psychology, 4,* 313–325.

Anderson, L., & Krathwohl, D. R. (2001). *Taxonomy for learning, teaching and assessing: A revision of Bloom's taxonomy of educational objectives.* New York: Longman.

Anglin, G., Towers, R., & Levie, W. (1996). Visual message design and learning: The role of static and dynamic illustrations. In *Handbook of Research for Instructional technology.* New York: Macmillan.

Arbinger Institute. (2002). *Leadership and self-deception: Getting out of the box.* San Francisco: Berrett-Koehler.

Atkins, S., & Murphy, K., (1993). Reflection: A review of the literature. *Journal of Advanced Nursing, 18,* 1188–1192.

Barnitz, J. G. (1986). Toward understanding the effects of cross-cultural schemata and discourse structure on second language reading comprehension. *Journal of Reading Behavior, 18,* 95–113.

Barron, A., & Atkins, D. (1994). Audio instruction in multimedia education: Is textual redundancy important? *Journal of Educational Multimedia and Hypermedia, 3,* 295–306.

Beary, R. P. (1994, March). Inquiring trainers want to know. *Training and Development.* 22–25.

Bernthal, P., Colteryahn, K., Davis, P., Naughton, J., Rothwell, W., & Wellins, R. (2004). *ASTD 2004 Competency study mapping the future: New workplace learning and performance competencies.* Alexandria, VA: American Society for Training and Development.

Boyd, E. M., & Fales, A. W. (1983). Reflective learning: Key to learning from experience. *Journal of Humanistic Psychology, 23,* 99–117.

Instructor Competencies: Standards for Face-to-Face, Online, and Blended Settings, pages 91–96
Copyright © 2004 by Information Age Publishing
All rights of reproduction in any form reserved.

Brady, F. N. (1990). *Ethical management, rules and results.* New York: Macmillan.

Collins, A., Brown, J. S., & Newman, S. E. (1989). Cognitive apprenticeship: Teaching the crafts of reading, writing, and mathematics. In L. B. Resnick (Ed.), *Knowing, learning, and instruction: Essays in honor of Robert Glaser* (pp. 453–494). Hillsdale, NJ: Erlbaum.

Collison, G., Elbaum, B., Haavind, S., & Tinker, R. (2000). *Facilitating online learning: Effective strategies for moderators.* Madison, WI: Atwood.

Cook, J. H. A., & Timmis, S.E. (2002) *Towards a theory of student motivation in virtual learning.* Association of Learning Technology.

Davis, E. (1998). *Scaffolding students' reflection for science learning.* Unpublished doctoral dissertation, University of California, Berkeley.

Dempsey, J. V., & Sales, G. C. (1993). *Interactive instruction and feedback.* NJ: Educational Technology Publications.

Dewey, J. (1933). *How we think: A restatement of the relation of reflective thinking to the educative process.* Chicago: Henry Regnery.

Dewey, J. (1938). *Experience and education.* New York: Macmillan.

DiVesta, F. J. (1989). Applications of cognitive psychology to education. In M.C. Wittrock & F. Farley (Eds.), *The future of educational psychology.* Hillsdale, NJ: Erlbaum.

Dörner, D. (1996). *The logic of failure: Why things go wrong and what we can do to make them right.* New York: Holt.

Dubois, D. D., & Rothwell, W. J. (2004). *Competency-based human resource management.* Palo Alto, CA: Davies-Black.

Duffy, T. M., & Cunningham, D. J. (1996). Constructivism: Implications for the design and delivery of instruction. In D. Jonassen (Ed), *Handbook of research for educational communications and technology.* New York: Macmillan.

Dwyer, F. M. (1978). *Strategies for improving visual learning.* State College, Pennsylvania: Learning Sciences.

Eitington, J. E. (1996). *The winning trainer: Winning ways to involve people in learning* (3rd ed.). Houston, TX: Gulf.

Flynn A. E., & Klein, J. D. (2001). The influence of discussion groups in a case-based learning environment. *Educational Technology, Research and Development, 49*(3), 69–84.

Foxon, M., Richey, R. C., Roberts, R., & Spannaus, T. W. (2003). *Training manager competencies: The standards.* Syracuse, NY: ERIC Clearinghouse on Information & Technology.

Gagné, R. M. (1985). *The conditions of learning* (4th ed.). New York: Holt, Rinehart, and Winston.

Gagné, R. M., & Merrill, M. D. (1990). Integrative goals for instructional design. *Educational Technology Research and Development, 38*(1), 23–30.

Gagné, R. M., & Medsker, K. L. (1996). *The Conditions of learning: Training applications.* FL: Harcourt Brace.

Ganesan, R. (2004). *Perceptions and practices of expert teachers in technology-based distance and distributed learning environments.* Unpublished Dissertation, Syracuse University, Syracuse.

Geis, G. L. (1986). Human performance technology: An overview. In M. E. Smith (Ed.), *Introduction to performance technology* (Vol. 1.). Washington, DC: National Society for Performance and Instruction.

Gilley, J., Geis, G., & Seyfer, C. (1987). Let's talk certification: Questions and answers for the profession about the profession. *Performance and Instruction, 26*(2), 7–17.

Goodyear, P. (2000). Environments for lifelong learning: Ergonomics, architecture and educational design. In J. M. Spector & T. M. Anderson (Eds.), *Integrated and holistic perspectives on learning, instruction and technology: Understanding complexity* (pp. 1–18). Dordrecht: Kluwer.

Goodyear, P., Salmon, G., Spector, J. M., Steeples, C., & Tickner, S. (2001). Competences for online teaching: A special report. *Educational Technology Research & Development, 49*(1), 65–72.

Grabowski, B., Suciati, & Pusch, W. (1990). Social and intellectual value of computer-mediated communications in a graduate community. *Educational & Training Technology International, 27*(3), 276–283.

Griffith, B. A., & Frieden, G. (2000). Facilitating reflective thinking in counselor education. *Counselor Education and Supervision, 40*, 80–93.

Hartley J. (1985): *Designing instructional text*. London: Kogan Page.

Henri, F., & Lundgren-Cayrol, K. (2001). *Apprentissage collaboratif à distance. Pour comprendre et concevoir des environnements d'apprentissage virtuels*. Sainte-Foy, Quebec, Canada: Presses de l'Université du Québec.

Hooghiemstra, T. (1992). Integrated management of human resources. In A. Mitrani, M. Dalziel, & D. Fitt (Eds.), *Competency based human resource management* (pp. 17–46). London: Kogan Page.

Hutchison, C., Shepherd, J., & Stein, F. (1988). *Instructor competencies: The standards*. Chicago: International Board of Standards for Training, Performance and Instruction.

Imel, S. (1992). *Reflective practice in adult education* (ERIC Digest No. 122 ED346319). Columbus OH: ERIC Clearinghouse on Adult Career and Vocational Education. Retrieved June 11, 2004, from http://www.ericfacility.net/ericdigests/ed346319.html

International Board of Standards for Training, Performance and Instruction. (1993). *Instructor competencies: The standards*. Batavia, IL: Author.

Jonassen, D. H. (1986). Hypertext principles for text and courseware design. *Educational Psychologist, 21*(4), 269–292.

Jonassen, D. H., Hernandez-Serrano, J., & Choi, I. (2000). Integrating constructivism and learning technologies. In J. M. Spector & T. M. Anderson (Eds.), *Integrated and holistic perspectives on learning, instruction and technology: Understanding complexity* (pp. 103–128). Dordrecht: Kluwer.

Keller, J. M. (1983). Motivational design of instruction. In C. M. Reigeluth (Ed.), *Instructional-design theories and models*. Hillsdale, NJ: Erlbaum.

Keller, J. M. (1987). The systematic process of motivational design. *Performance and Instruction, 26*(10), 1–8.

Kinchin, I. M., & Hay, D. B. (2000). How a qualitative approach of concept map analysis can be used to aid learning by illustrating patterns of conceptual development. *Educational Research, 42*(1), 43–58.

Klein, J. D. (2002, April). *Strategies for active learning*. Invited address presented at the University of Twente, The Netherlands.

Klein, J. D., & Doran, M. S. (1999). Implementing individual and small group learning structures with a computer simulation. *Educational Technology, Research & Development, 47*(1), 97–109.

Klein, J. D., & Rushby, N. (in press). Professional organizations and publications in instructional design and technology. In R. A. Reiser & J. V. Dempsey (Eds.). *Trends and issues in instructional design and technology*. Upper Saddle River, NJ: Merrill-Prentice Hall.

Knowles, M. S., Holton, E. F., & Swanson, R. A. (1998). *The adult learner: the definitive classic in adult education and human resource development,* Houston, TX: Gulf.

Ko, S., & Rossen, S. (2001). *Teaching online: A practical guide.* Boston: Houghton Mifflin.

Koszalka, T., Song, H., & Grabowski, B. (2002). Learners' perceptions of design factors found in problem-based learning (PBL) that support reflective thinking. *Proceedings for the 2001 Association for Educational Communications and Technology, 1,* 217–221.

Kulhavy, R. W., & Stock, W. A. (1989). Feedback in written instruction: The place of response certitude. *Educational Psychology Review, 1*(4), 279–308.

Land, S. M., & Hannafin, M. J. (1998, February). Learning with open-ended technology environments: Problems and issues. *Proceedings of the Association for Educational Communications and Technology,* St. Louis, MO.

Lapidus, T. (2000). *High impact training: Getting results and respect.* San Francisco: Jossey-Bass/Pfeiffer.

Lucia, A. D., & Lepsinger, R. (1999). *The art and science of competency models: Pinpointing critical success factors in organizations.* San Francisco: Jossey-Bass/Pfeiffer.

Marrelli, A.F. (1998). An introduction to competency analysis and modeling. *Performance Improvement, 37*(5), 8–17.

McCoy, C. (2004). *Selected glossary of training terms.* Retrieved June 11, 2004, from http://www.mccoytraining.com/glossary.html#4

McLagan, P.A. (May, 1997). Competencies: The next generation. *Training & Development,* 40–47.

Merrill, M. D., Li, Z., & Jones, M. (1991). Instructional transaction theory: An introduction. *Educational Technology, 31*(6), 7

Milrad, M., Spector, J. M., & Davidsen, P. I. (2000). Building and using simulation based environments for learning about complex domains. In R. Robson (Ed.), *MSET/2000 Conference Proceedings* (pp. 304–308). Charlottesville, VA: Association for the Advancement of Computing in Education.

Moon, J. (1999). *Reflection in learning and professional development: Theory and practice.* London: Kogan Page

Morecroft, J. D. W., & Sterman, J. D. (1994). *Modeling for learning organizations.* Portland, OR: Productivity Press.

Paquette, G. (2002). *L'ingénierie pédagogique: pour construire l'apprentissage en réseau.* Sainte-Foy, Quebec, Canada: Presses de l'Université du Québec.

Parry, S. B. (1998, June). Just what is a competency? (And why should you care?). *Training, 35*(6), 58–64.

Pavio, A. (1990). *Mental representations: A dual coding approach* (2nd ed.). New York: Oxford University Press.

Pea, R. D. (1985). Beyond amplification: Using the computer to reorganize mental functioning. *Educational Psychologist, 20*(4), 167–182.

Reeves, T. C., & Hedberg, J. G. (2003). *Interactive learning systems evaluation.* Englewood Cliffs, NJ: Educational Technology Publications.

Richey, R., Fields, D., & Foxon, M. (2001). *Instructional design competencies: The standards* (3rd ed.). Syracuse, NY: ERIC Clearinghouse on Information & Technology.

Romiszowski, A. J. (1999). *Designing instructional systems: Decision making in course planning and curriculum design.* Instructional Development Series.

Rosenberg, M. J. (2001). *e-Learning: Strategies for delivering knowledge in the digital age.* New York: McGraw-Hill.

Rothwell, W. (2002). *The workplace learner: How to align training initiatives with individual learning competencies.* New York: Amacom.

Salmon, G. (2000). E-*Moderating: The key to teaching and learning online.* London: Kogan Page.

Schön, D. A. (1987). *Educating the reflective practitioner.* San Francisco: Jossey-Bass.

Schön, D. A. (1991). *The reflective turn: Case studies in and on education practice.* New York: Teachers College Press.

Seels, B. B., & Richey, R. C. (1994). *Instructional technology: The definition and domains of the field.* Washington, DC: Association for Educational Communications and Technology.

Senge, P. (1990). *The fifth discipline: The art and practice of the learning organization.* New York: Doubleday.

Simon, H. A. (1972). Theories of bounded rationality. In C. B. McGuire & R. Radner (Eds.), *Decision and organization.* Amsterdam: North-Holland.

Spector, J. M. (2000, Fall). Trends and issues in educational technology: How far we have not come. *Update Semiannual Bulletin, 21*(2). Syracuse, NY: ERIC Information Technology Clearinghouse.

Spector, J. M., & Anderson, T. M. (2000). *Integrated and holistic perspectives on learning, instruction and technology: Understanding complexity.* Dordrecht: Kluwer.

Spector, J. M., & De la Teja, I. (2001, December). *Competencies for online teaching* (ERIC Digest EDO-IR-2001-09). Syracuse, NY: ERIC Information Technology Clearinghouse. Available at http://www.ericit.org/digests/EDO-IR-2001-09.shtml

Spector, J. M., & Edmonds, G. S. (2002, September). *Knowledge management in instructional design* (ERIC Digest EDO-IR-2002-02). Syracuse, NY: ERIC Clearinghouse for Information & Technology.

Spector, J. M., & Wang, X. (2002). Integrating technology into learning and working: Introduction. *Education, Technology and Society* [Online serial], *5*(1). Available at http://ifets.ieee.org/periodical/vol_1_2002/v_1_2002.html

Spencer, L. M., & Spencer, S. M. (1993). *Competence at work: Models for superior performance.* New York: Wiley.

Spiro, R. J., Coulson, R. L., Feltovich, P. J., & Anderson, D. (1988). Cognitive flexibility theory: Advanced knowledge acquisition in ill-structured domains. In V. Patel (Ed.), *Proceedings of the 10th Annual Conference of the Cognitive Science Society* (pp. 375–383). Hillsdale, NJ: Erlbaum.

Spiro, R. J., & Jehng, J. (1990). Cognitive flexibility and hypertext: Theory and technology for the non-linear and multidimensional traversal of complex subject matter. In D. Nix & R. Spiro (Eds.), *Cognition, education, and multimedia.* Hillsdale, NJ: Erlbaum.

Suessmuth, P., & Strengels, M. (1972, May). Wake them up–ask the right questions. *Training in Business and Industry,* 33.

Terry, R W. (1993). *Authentic leadership: Courage in action.* San Francisco: Jossey-Bass.

U.S. Department of Defense. (1999). *Department of Defense handbook: Glossary for training* (Part 4 MIL-HKBK-29612-4A). Washington, DC: Author.

Virtanen, P. J., Kosunen, E. A-L., Holmberg-Marttila, D. M. H., & Virjo, I. O. (1999). What happens in PBL tutorial sessions? An analysis of medical students' written accounts. *Medical Teacher, 21*(3), 270–276.

Visser, L., Plomp. Tj., Amirault, R., &. Kuiper W. J. A. M. (2002). Motivating students at a distance: The case of an international audience. *Educational Technology Research and Development 50*(2), 54–110.

Wallace, S. A., & Hagler, R. W. (1979). Knowledge of performance and the learning of a closed-motor skill. *Research Quarterly, 50,* 265–271.

Wiley, D. A. (2002). *Instructional Use of Learning Objects.* Bloomington, IN: Agency for Instructional Technology.

Williams, M. (1996). Learner control and instructional technologies. In Jonassen, D. (Ed.) *Handbook of research for educational communications and technology* (pp. 957–983). New York: Macmillan Library Reference.

Wittgenstein, L. (1921). *Tractatus Logico-Philosophicus.* London: Humanities Press.

Wittrock, M. C. (1974). Learning as a generative process. *Educational Psychologist, 11,* 87–95.

Wittrock, M. C. (1990). Generative processes of comprehension. *Educational Psychologist, 24,* 345–376.

Wlodkowski, R. (1998). *Enhancing adult motivation to learn.* San Francisco: Jossey-Bass.

THE 1993 IBSTPI INSTRUCTOR COMPETENCIES[1]

Competency 1: Analyze course materials and learner information.

(a) Review materials and audience information.
(b) Make minor adjustments to learning materials.
(c) Judge the appropriateness and adequacy of any adjustments.
(d) State a rationale for the judgment and adjustments.

Competency 2: Ensure preparation of the instructional site.

(a) Confirm logistical arrangements.
(b) Confirm the physical arrangement of the instructional site, materials, equipment, and furniture.
(c) Control the physical environment.
(d) Plan ways to minimize distractions.
(e) Ensure proper disposition of equipment, materials, and furniture.
(f) Judge how well logistical and physical arrangements support the instruction.

Competency 3: Establish and maintain instructor credibility.

(a) Demonstrate acceptable personal conduct.
(b) Demonstrate acceptable social practices.
(c) Demonstrate content expertise.
(d) Provide a model for professional and interpersonal behavior.
(e) Demonstrate flexibility in response to learner needs and interests.

Instructor Competencies: Standards for Face-to-Face, Online, and Blended Settings, pages 97–100
Copyright © 2004 by Information Age Publishing
All rights of reproduction in any form reserved.

(f) Judge the degree to which credibility is an issue or distraction at any time during instruction.
(g) State a rationale for the judgment and the actions taken to establish, maintain, and reestablish credibility in a particular situation or in general.

Competency 4: Manage the learning environment.

(a) Select initial presentation strategies.
(b) Involve learners in establishing an appropriate level of learner comfort.
(c) Adapt delivery to account for learner characteristics.
(d) Manage time available for course.
(e) Provide opportunities for learner success.
(f) Manage group interactions and participation.
(g) Resolve learner behavior problems.
(h) Judge whether the learning environment facilitates successful performance.
(i) State a rationale for the judgment.

Competency 5: Demonstrate effective communication skills.

(a) Use appropriate verbal and nonverbal language.
(b) Adapt verbal and nonverbal messages to learners' needs.
(c) Use frames of reference familiar to the learners.
(d) Determine if learners understand messages.
(e) Judge the effectiveness of the communication.
(f) State a rationale for the judgment.

Competency 6: Demonstrate effective presentation skills.

(a) Use the voice effectively.
(b) Use eye contact effectively.
(c) Use gestures, silence, movement, posture, space, and props effectively.
(d) Organize content effectively.
(e) Use anecdotes, stories, analogies, and humor effectively.
(f) Judge the effectiveness of a presentation.
(g) State a rationale for the judgment.

Competency 7: Demonstrate effective questioning skills and techniques.

(a) Use appropriate question types and levels.
(b) Direct questions appropriately.
(c) Use active listening techniques.
(d) Repeat, rephrase, or restructure questions.

(e) Provide opportunity and adequate time for learners to state questions, comments, and concerns and respond to questions.
(f) Judge the adequacy of instructional questions.
(g) State a rationale for the judgment.

*Competency 8: Respond appropriately to learners' needs for clarification or
feedback.*

(a) Identify learners with clarification and feedback needs.
(b) Determine when and how to respond.
(c) Provide prompt, timely, and specific feedback.
(d) Judge the adequacy of feedback and responses.
(e) State a rationale for the judgment.

Competency 9: Provide positive reinforcement and motivational incentives.

(a) Match learning outcomes to learner and organizational needs and
goals.
(b) Use introductory activities appropriate to developing learner
motivation.
(c) Plan and deliberately use feedback and reinforcement during
instruction.
(d) Judge the adequacy and appropriateness of motivational strategies
used during instruction.
(e) State a rationale for the judgment.

Competency 10: Use instructional methods appropriately.

(a) Implement a variety of standard instructional methods.
(b) Manage the group dynamics associated with each method.
(c) Employ instructional techniques appropriate to methods and
instructional situations prescribed.
(d) Judge the appropriateness and effectiveness of methods and
techniques.
(e) State a rationale for the judgment.

Competency 11: Use media effectively.

(a) Use media and hardware properly.
(b) Trouble-shoot minor hardware and other simple problems.
(c) Substitute for, add to, switch, or create media as required.
(d) Judge the effectiveness of the use of media.
(e) State a rationale for the judgment.

Competency 12: Evaluate learner performance.

(a) Monitor learner progress during instruction.
(b) Administer tests and instruments.
(c) Evaluate attainment of end-of-course objectives.
(d) Judge the adequacy of the evaluation.
(e) State a rationale for the judgment.

Competency 13: Evaluate delivery of instruction.

(a) Evaluate the instructional design, as modified, during instruction.
(b) Evaluate an instructor's performance.
(c) Evaluate the effects of other variables, including the instructional environment, on learner accomplishments.
(d) Judge how well a course works for a particular group of learners in a particular situation.
(e) State a rationale for the judgment.

Competency 14: Report evaluation information.

(a) Prepare to report post-course summary and evaluation information.
(b) Report evaluation and end-of-course information.
(c) Recommend revisions and changes to existing materials and suggestions for new programs and activities.
(d) Report information about learning and physical environments.
(e) Judge the adequacy, appropriateness, and timeliness of reports to instructional designers and appropriate management.
(f) State a rationale for both the information included in evaluation and summary reports and the audiences to receive that information.

NOTE

1. The 1993 ibstpi instructor competencies and performance statements are copyrighted by the International Board of Standards for Training, Performance and Instruction (ibstpi). All rights reserved.

THE IBSTPI CODE OF ETHICS FOR INSTRUCTORS[1]

The International Board of Standards for Training, Performance and Instruction (ibstpi) has adopted the following statement of ethical standards for instructors:

> Competent instructors comply with established ethical and legal standards. They ensure that all learners are treated fairly and that their right to confidentiality is respected. They avoid conflicts of interest and respect intellectual property including copyright. Furthermore, they comply with organizational and professional codes of ethics and recognize the implications of their instructional practices.

BACKGROUND

A fundamental ethical consideration that an instructor should contemplate is the question "Do I have the necessary knowledge, skills, and attitudes to teach the defined audience the assigned content effectively so that goals and objectives are met?" If there are questions regarding competence in the content domain, there is marginal probability that learners will be successful in meeting expected goals and objectives, and the organization's instructional program is, therefore, in jeopardy. Consequently, instructors should address this fundamental ethical question with regard to their abil-

Instructor Competencies: Standards for Face-to-Face, Online, and Blended Settings, pages 101–106
Copyright © 2004 by Information Age Publishing
All rights of reproduction in any form reserved.

ity to fulfill commitments and implied promises to meet the expectations of learners and employers.

In addition to an obligation to keep commitments and promises, there are other ethical considerations involving issues such as confidentiality, privacy and fairness. Instructors should make it clear to learners and employers that their integrity, honesty, fairness, and their respect for confidentiality and privacy are above reproach. Instructors should demonstrate equal respect for all people regardless of ethnicity, gender, nationality, and other differences. An ethical instructor engenders trust. While these statements appear both simple and obvious, the evidence collected in the extensive survey on which this set of competencies is based suggests that some instructors do not think seriously about their ethical obligations. The Board believes that instructors do have ethical obligations to learners and other individuals, to employers and organizations, to their profession and professional associations, to society, and to themselves. These obligations are based on their roles as instructors and the responsibilities and commitments associated with these roles.

INSTRUCTOR ROLES

There are multiple roles in which an instructor serves. Traditional instructor roles include being content experts, lesson and course organizers, activity schedulers, and evaluators. Instructors also serve as leaders not only in an instructional setting but in other contexts as well (Arbingder Institute, 2002; Lapidus, 2000). Instructors are responsible not only for improving the knowledge, skills, and attitudes of learners but also for positioning them for success in subsequent activities. Instructors often provide a role model for success within a particular profession or content domain. Many times, these roles expand to include advising and counseling in personal matters as well as professional matters.

RESPONSIBILITIES TO LEARNERS

Foremost among an instructor's responsibilities are obligations to learners. These obligations include providing learners with guidance and support in achieving instructional goals. They extend further to include respecting the rights of learners and being fair in all aspects of instruction to all learners. The rights of learners vary somewhat from one context to another. It is the instructor's responsibility to be familiar with these rights and to ensure that learners know their rights as well. Instructors should also be sensitive to their multiple roles and to the expectations of learners that derive from these multiple roles. In some cases, these roles are negotiated with individual learners. Regardless, it is generally advisable to make the responsibilities associated with roles explicit. When a learner raises an ethical issue, an ethical instructor listens first and then gathers any additional evidence that may be required and may consult with others before reaching a decision. Moreover, when an instructor's decision is challenged or changed, the instructor should continue to treat all those involved fairly and without bias.

RESPONSIBILITIES TO OTHER INDIVIDUALS

While the primary role of an instructor involves learners, instructors interact with others; there are responsibilities associated with these interactions. Instructors may be part of a teaching team and have obligations to the other members of the team. Some instructors have assistants to whom they are obligated to treat with the rights and responsibilities associated with an employer–employee relationship. Instructors have ethical responsibilities to their employers that include the accurate reporting of progress and problems to supervisors and managers. Finally, instructors have responsibilities to themselves. No person should be asked to do something that violates a personal sense of right and wrong. If an instructor believes that his or her personal ethics are compromised in a particular situation, the ethical instructor will make this known to others involved and do everything possible to avoid the conflict, including removing him- or herself from the situation.

RESPONSIBILITIES TO ORGANIZATIONS

Instructors nearly always work for an organization of one kind or another. In additional to the contractual obligations associated with employment, instructors have ethical responsibilities to their employing organizations just as those organizations have ethical responsibilities to instructors and other employees (e.g., advising employees of rights, grievance procedures, problematic behavior, etc.). Among an instructor's responsibility to the organization are fairly representing that organization to learners and others, accurately reporting outcomes to the organization, and maintaining the confidentiality of organizational records. A general guideline is to treat organizations in much the same way that one would treat an individual. For example, just as it would be wrong to spread false rumors about an individual, it is wrong to spread false rumors about an organization.

There are some situations where an instructor might have to decide whether responsibilities to individuals outweigh responsibilities to organizations, although it is rarely the same kinds of responsibilities that give rise to such quandaries. The safety and well-being of an individual is different from the safety and well-being of an organization; while such a conflict may be unlikely, the safety and well-being of an individual is likely to take precedence.

RESPONSIBILITIES TO SOCIETY

Instructors exist alongside learners and employers as citizens and members of society. As such, they have certain rights and responsibilities. It is unlikely that responsibilities to society would conflict with an instructor's other responsibilities, but it is worth keeping social responsibilities in mind as they provide a context for actions, decisions, and responsibilities. Part of an individual's identity is based on that individual's social setting. This is true for both learners and instructors. An instructor may encounter a wide diversity of learners, some of whom may come from different cultures and be accustomed to different societies. Moreover, different individuals may perceive their social responsibilities differently. Again, the general guideline is to make roles and responsibilities explicit whenever possible.

RESPONSIBILITY TO THE PROFESSION

Instructors may belong to multiple professional communities, including a community associated with the content domain as well as an educational community. These communities typically have professional associations that have formulated their own ethical codes. Certainly those codes should be respected if one wishes to remain a respected member of that professional community. Instructors have a particular obligation to represent the education and training community in a positive way. If an instructor is unethical or incompetent, harm is done to other members of the instructional community. Learners may come to distrust or resent other instructors based on the inadequacies of one. On the other hand, if an instructor is highly competent and a model of integrity, learners are likely to hold other instructors in higher esteem.

A PRACTICAL FRAMEWORK FOR ETHICS

According to Terry (1993), it is impossible to lead without being ethical. Those in leadership positions who engage in unethical actions cannot be effective role models and cannot sustain a vision of progress and performance for an organization. The same can be said about being an instructor. Like many others, instructors are required to balance rules and results, rights and responsibilities, progress and promises. Tensions and conflicting considerations may arise. It is how one avoids or resolves conflicts that reflect one's ethics. Is it possible to provide more than high-sounding advice to help instructors be sensitive to their ethical obligations? What follows is a practical framework that may prove useful to some instructors.

Instructors, like other professionals, require tools for analysis and many instructional activities. Instructors should make their ethical perspectives explicit and then analyze and reflect on them. There are tools that can be useful in this process. Instructors should also assist learners in discovering their own ethical perspectives. Without a systematic and reliable method for examining individual ethical perspectives, decisions become difficult and often arbitrary.

One tool that we recommend is the "Survey of Ethical Theoretic Aptitudes," which is called "The Brady Inventory" by many practitioners (see Brady, 1990). This survey or inventory provides instructors and learners with valuable information regarding their personal ethical perspective. They are provided with an insight into how and why they make ethical decisions. Moreover, the Brady Inventory provides instructors and learners with a benchmark from which they not only make ethical decisions, but gain an understanding of how they and why others make ethical decisions. This ethical inventory can be widely applied in many settings, which is why it is cited here. Other such tools can be found that may provide consistency and insight into ethical decision making that ibstpi encourages.

There are many approaches, methods, or schemes for systematically working one's way through ethical problems or dilemmas. Having a tool such as the Brady Inventory on hand enables an instructor to listen and analyze and possibly collect additional evidence and advice before making a decision or taking action. In this sense, the ethical guideline is exactly the opposite of the popular adage that "he who hesitates is lost." Brady's framework also provides easily accessible terminology (e.g., rules and results) as well as general categories for personal ethical perspectives (e.g., formalist or utilitarian). The value of the terminology and categories is that it provides a framework within which one might evaluate one's thoughts about what is right or wrong in various situations. These can then be discussed with others.

CONCLUSION

Instructors exist in a changing world and have many different roles and responsibilities. Instructors will continue to be held responsible for subject matter content, for classroom management, for scheduling, and for assessment. Instructors have other roles that also have associated ethical responsibilities, including being an advisor, being an employee, and being a leader. It is challenging and important to be a competent instructor. It is no less challenging and no less important to be an ethical instructor.

NOTE

1.   This code of ethics was written with Dennis Fields, a former member of ibstpi and Professor at St. Cloud State University, and with Jan Visser, an ibstpi member and President of the Learning Development Institute.

APPENDIX C

RESOURCES
FOR INSTRUCTORS[1]

The International Board of Standards for Training, Performance and Instruction (ibstpi) believes that a competent instructor is someone who continually updates and improves their own professional knowledge and skills. Every instructor should stay abreast of current principles of learning and instruction, update their technology skills, establish and maintain professional contacts, and participate in professional development activities. The resources described in this appendix are intended to assist instructors in these endeavors. Below, we provide information about the professional associations, conferences, journals, digital repositories, electronic forums, and noteworthy books that may be of interest to instructors who work in face-to-face, online, or blended settings throughout the world. Readers who want more detailed information about professional organizations and journals in the field should consult Klein and Rushby (in press).

PROFESSIONAL ASSOCIATIONS

Academy of Human Resource Development (AHRD) encourages the systematic study of human resource development. http://www.ahrd.org

American Educational Research Association (AERA) is concerned with improving education by encouraging scholarly inquiry. http://www.aera.net

Instructor Competencies: Standards for Face-to-Face, Online, and Blended Settings, pages 107–117
Copyright © 2004 by Information Age Publishing
All rights of reproduction in any form reserved.

Associação Brasileira de Educação a Distância (ABED) is interested in research, development, and promotion of distance education. http://www.abed.org.br

Association for Learning Technology (ALT) endorses good practice in the use of learning technology in education and industry and fosters collaboration between practitioners, researchers, and policymakers. http://www.alt.ac.uk

American Society for Training and Development (ASTD) provides leadership to individuals and organizations that are committed to workplace learning and performance. http://astd.org

Association for the Advancement of Computing in Education (AACE) is dedicated to the improvement of learning and teaching with information technology. http://www.aace.org

Association for Applied Interactive Multimedia (AAIM) supports professionals who use and develop interactive multimedia for education and training. http://www.aaim.org

Association for Educational Communications and Technology (AECT) links professionals holding a common interest in the use of educational technology and its application to the learning process. http://www.aect.org

Association for Media and Technology in Education in Canada (AMTEC) is a pan-Canadian community of educators, media producers, researchers, librarians, and other professionals who work to facilitate and improve learning through the appropriate application and integration of educational technology. http://www.amtec.ca

Australasian Society for Computers in Learning in Tertiary Education (ASCILITE) is a society for those involved in tertiary computer-based education and training, including educational interactive multimedia. http://www.ascilite.org.au

Australian Council for Computers in Education (ACCE) is a professional body for those involved in the use of learning technology in education that strives to encourage and maintain a level of excellence in this field of endeavor throughout Australia. http://www.acce.edu.au

Australian Society for Educational Technology (ASET) is the Australian national organization for people with professional interests in educational technology. http://www.aset.org.au

British Learning Association (BLA) provides impartial information and advice on best practice, techniques, and technologies in learning. http://www.british-learning.com

Chartered Institute of Personnel and Development (CIPD) is a professional body for those involved in the management and development of people in the United Kingdom. http://www.cipd.co.uk

Computer Education Management Association (CeDMA) is a forum for managers and directors of computer education organizations to discuss issues in computer training and the technical training industry. http://www.cedma.org

Commonwealth of Learning is an intergovernmental organization fostering the development and sharing of open learning and distance education technologies. http://www.col.org

Distance Education Association of New Zealand (DEANZ) is made up of individual and institutional members from New Zealand and the Pacific Rim committed to fostering growth, development, research, and good practice in distance education, open learning, and flexible delivery systems for education. http://www.deanz.org.nz

Educational Research Association of Singapore (ERAS) promotes the practice and utilization of educational research with the view to enhancing the quality of education. http://eduweb.nie.edu.sg/eras

Emergent Learning Forum is a community of decision makers that promotes understanding and use of learning in industry and government worldwide. http://www.elearningforum.com

e-Learning Network is a source of information and best practice on design, implementation, and evaluation of electronic learning for users of technology in training in the United Kingdom. http://www.elearningnetwork.org

European Association for Research on Learning and Instruction (EARLI) provides a platform to exchange and discuss research on instruction, education, and training. http://www.earli.org

European Federation for Open and Distance Learning (EFODL) is a pan-European network for professionals involved in the development, distribution, and use of technology distance learning. http://www5 .vdab.be/vdab/test/efodl/top.htm

European Institute for e-Learning offers development and certification of competencies and quality assurance for learning services throughout Europe. http://www.qwiki.info

The Indian Society for Training and Development (ISTD) organizes training programs in India that cover selected areas of HRD with special emphasis on training, tools, and technologies. http://www.iftdo2004hrd .com/myweb5/favorite.htm

Institute of IT Training (IITT) is concerned with developing and promoting high standards of excellence for the training of information technology and the use of technology in training. http://www.iitt.org.uk

International Federation of Training and Development Organizations (IFTDO) is a worldwide network committed to identify, develop, and transfer knowledge, skills, and technology to enhance personal and organizational growth, human performance, and productivity. http://www.iftdo2004hrd.com/myweb5/interest.htm

International Forum of Educational Technology and Society (IFETS) encourages discussions on issues affecting educational system developers and education communities. http://ifets.ieee.org

International Society for Performance Improvement (ISPI) is dedicated to improving productivity and performance in the workplace through the application of human performance technology. http://ispi.org

International Society for Technology in Education (ISTE) provides leadership and service to improve teaching and learning by advancing the effective use of technology in K–12 education and teacher education. http://iste.org

International Technology Education Association (ITEA) is devoted to enhancing technology education through experiences in K–12 schools. http://www.iteawww.org

International Visual Literacy Association (IVLA) is concerned with issues dealing with education, instruction, and training in modes of visual communication and their application through the concept of visual literacy. http://ivla.org

Korean Society for Educational Technology (KSET) is concerned with improving learning environments and solving real-life learning problems with educational technology. http://203.246.105.157/php/e_index.php3

National Association of Distance Education Organizations in South Africa (NADEOSA) promotes access to lifelong learning through the belief that distance education methods can play a major role in resolving South Africa's educational challenges. http://www.nadeosa.org.za

Open and Distance Learning Association of Australia (ODLAA) aims to advance the practice and study of distance education in Australia, foster communication between distance educators, and maintain links with other professional associations. http://www.odlaa.org

SANTEC—Educational Technology and eLearning for Development is a South African network of educational technology practitioners with an interest in educational technology and electronic learning in developing environments. http://www.santecnetwork.org

Society for Applied Learning Technology (SALT) is an organization for professionals whose work requires knowledge in the field of instructional technology. http://salt.org

Society for Information Technology and Teacher Education (SITE) is focused on the integration of instructional technologies into teacher education. http://site.aace.org

South African Institute of Distance Education (SAIDE) promotes open learning principles, the use of quality distance education methods, and the appropriate use of technology to assist in the reconstruction of education and training in South Africa http://www.saide.org.za

United Nations Educational, Science and Cultural Organization (UNESCO) promotes the exchange of ideas and international cooperation on issues related to education, science, culture, and communication. www.unesco.org

World Association for Online Education (WAOE) is an international virtual association of educators interested in online education as a professional discipline. http://www.waoe.org

JOURNALS

American Educational Research Journal

*American Journal of Distance Education*www.ajde.com

Asia Pacific Journal of Education

Australasian Journal of Educational Technology

Australian Educational Computing

Australian Educational Researcher

British Journal of Educational Psychology

British Journal of Educational Technology

Canadian Journal of Learning and Technology

Cognition and Instruction

Computers in Human Behavior

Contemporary Educational Psychology

Contemporary Issues in Technology and Teacher Education

Curriculum and Teaching

Distance Education

Distance Educator

Education and Information Technologies
Educational Practice and Theory
Educational Researcher
Educational Technology
Educational Technology and Society
Educational Technology Research and Development
Educational Technology Review
e-journal of Instructional Science and Technology
eLearn Magazine
Electronic Journal for the Integration of Technology in Education
European Educational Research Journal
European Journal of Open and Distance Learning
Evaluation and Program Planning
Higher Education Research and Development
Instructional Science
Interactive Educational Multimedia
Interactive Multimedia Electronic Journal of Computer-Enhanced Learning
International Journal on E-Learning
International Journal of Educational Technology
International Journal of Instructional Media
International Journal of Training and Development
International Journal of Training Research
International Review of Research in Open & Distance Learning
Journal of Asynchronous Learning Networks
Journal of Computer Assisted Learning
Journal of Computer-Mediated Communication
Journal of Computing in Teacher Education
Journal of Distance Education
Journal of Educational Computing Research
Journal of Educational Multimedia and Hypermedia
Journal of Educational Psychology
Journal of Educational Research
Journal of Educational Technology Systems
Journal of Experimental Education
Journal of Instruction Delivery Systems
Journal of Interactive Instruction Development
Journal of Interactive Learning Research
Journal of Interactive Media in Education

Journal of Interactive Online Learning
Journal of Online Behavior
Journal of Research on Technology in Education
Journal of Technology and Teacher Education
Journal of Technology Education
Journal of Technology Studies
Journal of Technology, Learning, and Assessment
Journal of the Learning Sciences
Journal of Visual Literacy
Learning and Instruction
Learning and Leading with Technology
Learning and Training Innovations
Learning Circuits
Mentoring and Tutoring
Online Journal of Distance Learning Administration
Open Learning
Performance Improvement Journal
Performance Improvement Quarterly
Perspectives in Quality Online Education
Practical Assessment, Research and Evaluation
Quarterly Review of Distance Education
Review of Educational Research
Revista Brasileira de Aprendizagem Aberta et a Distância
Revista de Educación a Distancia
Revista Iberoamericana de Educación/ Revista Ibero-Americana de Educaçao
Teachers and Teaching: Theory and Practice
Teaching with Technology Today
Technology and Learning
Technology Source
TechKnowLogia
Tech Trends
T.H.E. Journal
T & D Magazine
Training Magazine
Turkish Online Journal of Distance Education
Turkish Online Journal of Educational Technology
Wirtualna Edukacja

DIGITAL REPOSITORIES AND ELECTRONIC FORUMS

American Library Association (ALA) provides a database and offers Knowledge Quest and other resources. http://www.ala.org/ala/aasl/aaslpubsandjournals/kqweb/kqarchives/volume28/285Hall.htm

Association for the Advancement of Computing in Education (AACE) Digital Library allows users to search current and past issues of AACE journals. http://www.aace.org/DL/index.cfm

Bibliography on Computer Based Assessment and Distance Learning is a searchable collection of hundreds of references maintained by Sal Valenti, University of Ancona, Italy. http://liinwww.ira.uka.de/bibliography/Misc/cba.html

Campus Alberta Repository of Educational Objects (CAREO) is a searchable Web-based collection of multidisciplinary teaching materials. http://www.careo.org/

Center for Research on Evaluation, Standards, and Student Testing (CRESST) promotes evaluation testing techniques and provides its publications online with a page devoted to teachers. http://cresst96.cse.ucla.edu/index3.htm

Connexions provides a database of educational content modules and curricula from Rice University, including open-source software. http://cnx.rice.edu/

Discovery School is a guide for educators developed by Kathy Schrock that provides a categorized list of sites useful for enhancing curriculum and professional growth. http://school.discovery.com/schrockguide/index.html

Instructional Technology Council (ITC) provides a repository containing reports, distance education links, and related resources. http://144.162.197.250/default.htm

Distance Learning Resource Guide: Education and Technology Issues is a repository of articles, references, associations, and organizations related to distance learning. http://www.headstartinfo.org/infocenter/guides/dl_assoc.htm

Department of Education (DOE) provides many online resources, including instructional units and lesson plans, that help teachers to integrate the Internet into K–12 classroom instruction. http://www-ed.fnal.gov/doe

EDUCAUSE Information Resources is an international repository for information about managing and using information resources in higher education and includes a section devoted to distance education. http://www.educause.edu/ir/

EduSource is a pan-Canadian repository with a searchable collection of linked and interoperable learning objects. http://www.edusource .ca/english/home_eng.html

Educational Resources Information Center (ERIC) is a national information system funded by the U.S. Department of Education to provide access to education literature and resources. http://www.eric.ed.gov/

Gateway to Educational Materials (GEM) is a database of lesson plans, curriculum, units and educational materials at federal, state, university, nonprofit, and commercial websites. http://www.geminfo.org

International Centre for Distance Learning (ICDL) provides a literature database that contains bibliographic information on over 12,000 books, journal articles, research reports, conference papers, dissertations, and other types of literature relating to all aspects of the theory and practice of distance education. http://www-icdl.open.ac.uk

International Forum for Education, Technology and Society (IFETS) is affiliated with the IEEE Learning Technology Task Force and provides many resources of interest and relevance to teaching and learning with technology. http://ifets.ieee.org/

Instructional Technology Forum (ITFORUM) is an electronic listserv that promotes discussion of theories, research, new paradigms, and practices pertaining to instructional technology. http://it.coe.uga.edu/ itforum/index.html

LearnNB emerged from the New Brunswick eLearning Forum as a bilingual umbrella organization to promote the development of e-learning and knowledge technologies. http://www.learnnb.ca/

Learning Objects Portal provides links to learning object repositories and maintains a log pertaining to learning objects. http://ilearn.senecac .on.ca/lop/repositories/repositories.htm

Library Support Staff offers many online resources for those who teach online and in classroom settings. http://www.librarysupportstaff .com/onlineteach.html

Multimedia Educational Resource for Learning and Online Teaching (MERLOT) provides online resources for faculty and students of higher education. http://www.merlot.org

Massachusetts Institute of Technology (MIT) Open Courseware offers free search of websites, assignments, syllabi, and other pedagogical resources for MIT courses. http://ocw.mit.edu

National Education Association (NEA) offers educators access to various online teaching and learning resources. http://www.nea.org/he/abouthe/techip.html

Perseus is a digital library that facilitates interactions through time, space, and language in order to provide access to a wide range of source materials. http://www.perseus.tufts.edu/

Texas Educational Network (TENET) provides current and useful resources for the education community. http://www.tenet.edu/

Theory into Practice (TIP) is a database created by Greg Kearsley to make learning and instructional theory more accessible to educators. The database contains brief summaries of 50 major theories of learning and instruction. http://tip.psychology.org

Teaching, Learning and Technology Group (TLT) provides a variety of resources to help educational institutions, associations, and corporations around the world to improve teaching and learning. http://www.tltgroup.org/

WebQuest Page at San Diego State University includes resources for Bernie Dodge's WebQuest activities, which are inquiry-oriented learning experiences in which most or all of the information used by learners is drawn from the Web. http://webquest.sdsu.edu/

Wisconsin Online Resource Center (WORC) contains learning objects created at the Wisconsin Technical College for a wide variety of subjects. http://wisc-online.com

NOTEWORTHY BOOKS

Bandura, A. (1986). *Social foundations of thought and action.* Englewood Cliffs, NJ: Prentice-Hall.

Bloom, B. S., & Krathwohl, D. R. (1984). *Taxonomy of educational objectives: Handbook 1: Cognitive domain.* White Plains, NY: Longman.

Bransford, J. (1979). *Human cognition: Learning, understanding, and remembering.* Pacific Grove, CA: Brooks/Cole.

Bruner, J. S. (1966). *Toward a theory of instruction.* Cambridge, MA: Harvard University Press.

Dewey, J. (1938/1997). *Experience and education.* New York: Macmillan.

Gagné, R. M. (1985). *The conditions of learning* (4th ed.). New York: Holt, Rinehart & Winston.

Johnson, D. W., & Johnson, R. T. (1994). *Learning together and alone: Cooperative, competitive, and individualistic learning.* (4th ed.). Needham Heights, MA: Allyn & Bacon.

Jonassen, D. H. (1995). *Computers in the classroom: Mindtools for critical thinking.* Paramus, NJ: Prentice-Hall.

Kirkpatrick, D. L. (1994). *Evaluating training programs: The four levels.* San Francisco: Berrett-Koehler.

Knowles, M. S. (1980). *The modern practice of adult education: From pedagogy to andragogy.* Englewood Cliffs, NJ: Prentice Hall.

Mager, R. F. (1997). *Preparing instructional objectives: A critical tool in the development of effective instruction.* Atlanta, GA: Center for Effective Performance.

McKeachie, W. J. (1999). *Teaching tips: Strategies, research, and theory for college and university teachers.* Boston: Houghton Mifflin.

Merrill, M. D., Tennyson, R. D., & Posey, L. O. (1992). *Teaching concepts: An instructional design guide.* Englewood Cliffs, NJ: Educational Technology Publications.

Norman, D. A. (1993). *Things that make us smart: Cognitive artifacts as tools for thought.* Reading, MA: Addison Wesley Longman.

Perkins, D. N. (Ed.). (1997). *Software goes to school: Teaching for understanding with new technology.* New York: Oxford University Press.

Powers, B. (1992). *Instructor performance: Mastering the delivery of training.* San Francisco: Jossey-Bass.

Rossett, A., & Sheldon, K. (2001). *Beyond the podium: Delivering training and performance to a digital world.* San Francisco: Jossey-Bass.

Salomon, G. (1994). *Interaction of media, cognition, and learning: An exploration of how symbolic forms cultivate mental skills and affect knowledge acquisition.* Mahwah, NJ: Erlbaum.

Silverman, M. (2000). *The 2000 training & performance sourcebook.* New York: Ringbound/McGraw-Hill

Schank, R. C., & Cleary, C. (1995). *Engines for education.* Mahwah, NJ: Erlbaum.

Skinner, B. F. (1968). *Technology of teaching.* Paramus, NJ: Prentice Hall.

Vygotsky, L. S. (1978). *Mind in society.* Cambridge, MA: Harvard University Press.

NOTE

1. This list of resources was developed by Ileana de la Teja, James D. Klein, and J. Michael Spector.

APPENDIX D

GLOSSARY OF TERMS[1]

Access code
A password that provides access to a computer, software application, or network system. *Related term:* User ID.

Active learning
A strategy that involves learning by doing and provides opportunities for learners to meaningfully talk, listen, write, read, and reflect on instructional content.

Active listening
Paying close attention to what another person is communicating, including the unspoken messages, and reflecting back what has been understood.

Adaptive testing
An individualized assessment technique that automatically determines which questions are presented based on prior responses.

Anecdote
A short personal story, account, or observation often used as an instructional strategy to illustrate complex concepts or to promote motivation to learn.

Application setting
The context or situations in which knowledge, skills, and attitudes will be used.

Instructor Competencies: Standards for Face-to-Face, Online, and Blended Settings, pages 119–130
Copyright © 2004 by Information Age Publishing
All rights of reproduction in any form reserved.   119

Apprenticeship model

A one-on-one method of instruction that promotes the development of refined skills and deep understanding. *Related term:* On-the-job training.

Assessment

A measure of individual learning for various purposes, including a determination of readiness for learning, monitoring progress, and measuring achievement after instruction.

Assessment tool

A tool or instrument to measure learning and performance; typically includes tests, surveys, observation, or diagnostic checklists.

Asynchronous

A form of communication where interaction is delayed over time, using tools such as e-mail or threaded discussion.

Audience

The people for whom the instruction or message is intended. *Related terms:* Target group; Target population.

Authoring tool

A software application that enables users to create computer or Web-based course materials.

Autonomous learning

Learning in which individuals are responsible for and in control of their own learning process. *Related term:* Self-directed learning.

Best practice

A technique or method that is regarded as exemplary on the basis of experience or research.

Blended setting

An instructional setting that combines and integrates aspects of online and face-to-face instruction. *Related terms:* Hybrid setting; Blended solution.

Certification

The voluntary process by which a professional association or organization measures and reports on the degree of competence of individual practitioners (Gilley, Geis, & Seyfer, 1987).

Chat

A synchronous form of communication in which learners exchange ideas.

Chat room

An electronic meeting space used for real-time, message-based discussions.

Code of ethics

A set of principles intended to aid members of the field individually and collectively in maintaining a high level of professional conduct (Seels & Richey, 1994).

Cognitive science

An interdisciplinary field concerned with thinking, understanding, and mental processes.

Collaborative learning

An instructional strategy in which several learners work together to achieve a common goal.

Competency

A knowledge, skill, or attitude that enables one to effectively perform the activities of a given occupation or function to the standards expected in employment.

Community of practice

A group of professionals united by a common concern or purpose, dedicated to supporting each other in increasing their knowledge, creating new insights, and enhancing performance in a particular domain (Rosenberg, 2001). *Related terms:* Learning community; Knowledge community.

Conflict of interest

A situation in which personal business affairs may materially or adversely affect one's relationship with the organization.

Copyright

The right to copy or reproduce intellectual property.

Criticality

The perceived level of importance of a competency or performance statement.

Culture
The knowledge, values, and practices shared by a group.

Delivery system
The various means used to present instruction; may include a combination of lecture, workbook, Web-based training, interactive television broadcast, or other media.

Didactic instruction
A strategy in which learners are presented with information and are asked to respond to questions.

Discussion board
An electronic space for posting messages and replies about a specific topic. *Related terms:* Bulletin board; Discussion forum; Message board; Threaded discussion.

Distance education
An instructional setting in which learners and instructors are separated by location and/or time. *Related terms:* Distance learning; E-learning; Online learning.

Domain
A cluster of related competencies. Other uses: A subject matter area.

e-learning
The use of electronic technologies to deliver a broad array of solutions that enhance knowledge and performance (Rosenberg, 2001).

e-learning solutions
Instruction, information, and communication delivered via all electronic media including the Internet, Intranets, satellite broadcast, multimedia, audio/video tape, interactive TV, CD-ROM, and wireless devices.

Electronic signature
The electronic equivalent of a handwritten signature. Also used to confirm identity.

Emerging technologies
New techniques, tools, and equipment used in designing or delivering instruction, including virtual reality, reusable learning objects, wireless technologies, and multi-user object-oriented domains (adapted from Seels & Richey, 1994).

Emoticons

Special characters used as shorthand to express emotions.

Evaluation

The process of determining the adequacy, value, outcomes, and impact of instruction and learning (adapted from Seels & Richey, 1994).

Face-to-face instruction

A setting in which learners and instructors are in the same location at the same time.

Facilitation

The use of attending, observing, listening, and questioning skills to help a group of learners work together productively.

Feedback

Information provided to learners about their responses. Other use: Information provided to instructors, usually during evaluation.

Ground rules

The mutually agreed-upon rules governing behavior or actions in a given setting.

Human factors

The variables that impact human performance. *Related terms:* Human–computer interface; Ergonomics.

Hyperlink

A link in an electronic document connecting to other digital information. These links are usually represented by highlighted words or images. *Related term:* Hypertext.

Icebreaker

An activity presented at the beginning of instruction to engage learners and prepare them for interaction.

Individualized instruction

Instructional materials or activities that have been customized to account for individual learner characteristics and performance. *Related terms:* Adaptive instruction; Personalized instruction; Learner-centered instruction.

Information Technology (IT)

Hardware, software, services, infrastructure, and processes that allow an organization to make effective use of a variety of forms of data, information, and knowledge. *Related term:* Information and Communications Technology (ICT).

Instant messaging

The synchronous exchange of short text messages in an online setting. *Related term:* Text messaging.

Instruction

A planned process that facilitates learning and performance.

Instructional activity

A planned event intended to promote learning.

Instructional design

Systematic instructional planning including needs assessment, development, evaluation, implementation, and maintenance of materials and programs (adapted from Seels & Richey, 1994). *Related term:* Instructional systems design.

Instructional equipment

Tools such as computers, flip charts, and overhead projectors used to deliver or enhance the delivery of instruction.

Instructional materials

Resources such as participant notes, graphics, and posters used during instruction or training.

Instructional method

A component of the instructional strategy defining a particular means for accomplishing the objective (U.S. Department of Defense, 1999).

Instructional setting

The venue where instruction occurs whether face-to-face, online, or blended. *Related term:* Learning environment.

Instructional strategy

A plan that includes instructional activities and methods to sequence the learning and teach content with or without an instructor.

Instructional technology

A process, technique, tool, or device used in designing or delivering learning or performance solutions; typical instructional technologies include communications and information systems. *Related terms:* IT; Information Communications Technology (ICT).

Instructor

An individual responsible for activities intended to improve knowledge, skills, and attitudes, regardless of specific job title.

Instructor guide

A resource provided to the instructor that contains objectives, procedures, activities, and other information required for the successful implementation of the course. *Related terms:* Leader guide; Trainer guide; Training manual.

Intellectual property

The knowledge, processes, and capabilities that a company or an individual has developed; typically protected by copyright.

Intranet

A network that uses Internet-like systems, but which is closed to people outside the organization.

Learner-centered instruction

An instructional approach that places the learner's needs or requirements at the center of the decision-making process. *Related term:* Individualized instruction.

Learning

A relatively stable change in knowledge, performance, or attitude as a result of experience not attributable to maturation.

Learning management system (LMS)

A Web- or network-based system that enables learner and instructor interaction and provides such functions as learner tracking, competency management, grading, authoring, and report generation. *Related term:* Web-based course management system.

Learner motivation

An internal disposition toward learning that is demonstrated by effort and persistence.

Learning organization

An organization committed to continuous improvement and the integration of learning to improve organizational performance.

Learning paradigm

A view of learning based on established principles such as behaviorism, cognitivism, or social constructivism.

Learning theory

Concepts, constructs, principles, and propositions derived from research that describes how people learn.

Logistical arrangements

The activities pertaining to setting up and implementing a learning activity.

m-learning

The use of wireless personal communication devices such as pagers, cell phones, and personal digital assistants (PDAs) to deliver data and learning. *Related terms:* Mobile learning; Mobile training; Mobile e-learning

Media

The means by which instruction is presented to the learner; typically classified in terms of the perceptual channels employed, such as visual or auditory media. *Related terms:* Delivery media; Delivery systems.

Message

A meaningful unit of communication that may be written, visual, or oral. Messages may be instructional, informational, or motivational.

Motivational strategies

Actions taken by the instructor to increase learner effort and persistence.

Multimedia

The integration of various media to support training and performance improvement. The media may include graphics, video, animation, sound, and text.

Netiquette

The accepted guidelines for communicating electronically.

Organizational psychology

The study of individual and group behaviors in organizational settings.

On-the-job training (OJT)

A formal or informal program of instruction by subject-matter experts who coach, advise, and mentor workers in need of training while they are performing real job tasks (McCoy, 2004).

Online collaboration

An instructional strategy in which learners work together online in teams or groups to solve a problem, complete a project, or achieve a learning goal. *Related terms:* Cooperative learning; Collaborative learning.

Online instruction

Instruction delivered using the Web, Internet, or other distance technologies. *Related terms:* Online training; Web-based or Internet-based instruction.

Organizational context

The characteristics or culture of an organization that are relevant to learning and performance.

Organizational goals

The focus of an organization's efforts.

Participant guide

A resource provided to the participant that contains objectives, schedules of activities, and other information required for the successful completion of the course. *Related terms:* Participant materials; Trainee guide; Learner guide.

Password

A word or code known only to the user to restrict access.

Performance statement

A detailed explanation of activities comprising a competency statement.

Performance technology

The process of selection, analysis, design, development, implementation, and evaluation of programs to cost-effectively influence human behavior and accomplishment (Geis, 1986).

Portability

The ability to easily move a software application or resource from one platform or operating system to another.

Portfolio

A collection of work that documents the learner's performance over a given period; may contain original work as well as photographs, clippings, and documentation from various sources.

Presentation skills

The skills required to present or deliver instruction effectively; typically includes the ability to communicate effectively, facilitate discussion, use humor wisely, and adapt to group dynamics.

Professional credibility
The quality of being trustworthy and believable within one's professional setting.

Professional development
Activities that enhance the skill, knowledge, or capacity of the practitioner, including attending professional association meetings and conferences, reading relevant texts, and networking with other practitioners.

Professional foundations
Those competencies considered foundational to the field; the base competencies that underpin the field.

Proprietary information
Information that has value to a company and that is not public knowledge. *Related terms:* Intellectual property; Copyright.

Question types
Various question formats such as structured/unstructured or closed/open.

Real-time
The actual time at which an event occurs; typically applicable to synchronous learning activities.

Reflective practice
A mode that integrates or links thought and action with reflection. It involves thinking about and critically analyzing one's actions with the goal of improving one's professional practice (Imel, 1992).

Scaffolding
A tool that supports the learning of new skills or concepts; typically useful for novice learners.

Scoring rubric
A set of guidelines for assessing performance; usually a list of concise narrative statements against which performance is measured.

Server
Computer hardware that supports specific software applications accessed by multiple users; typically in a network environment.

Socratic method

An instructional method that relies on asking a series of questions designed to lead learners to discover knowledge rather than being told by the instructor.

Sophist tradition

An instructional approach usually associated with the lecture method.

Standards

Statements of expectations of performance or levels of knowledge in a specific content domain or job role.

Streaming

The transmission of large media files (graphics, video, or audio) across a network to an individual computer. *Related terms:* Audio streaming; Streaming video.

Subject-matter expert

A content specialist who advises or assists in instructional design. *Related terms:* SME; Content expert.

Synchronous

A form of communication where interaction occurs in real time, using tools such as video-conferencing and chat.

Text messaging

The asynchronous exchange of short text messages using a pager, smart phone, Personal Digital Assistant (PDA), or other wireless device. *Related terms:* Short Messaging Service (SMS); Instant messaging.

Threaded discussion

An electronic space that allows for a continuing dialog on a single topic. *Related term:* Discussion board.

Train-the-trainer course

A comprehensive course to develop instructor competence.

Training

Learning that is provided in order to improve workplace performance.

Training manager

Manager of the training function within an organization. Term may also be applied to managers of instructional design and development groups, or managers of instructors and trainers.

Transfer

The application of knowledge and skills acquired in an instructional setting to another environment, typically a work setting.

Usability

The measure of how effectively, efficiently, and easily a person can navigate an interface, find information on it, and achieve his or her goals (American Society for Training and Development, 2004).

Video-conferencing

A form of synchronous communication using video and audio to support discussion between groups in different locations.

Visuals

Graphics or teaching materials that pictorially describe ideas or convey meaning, and include items such as overhead transparencies, screen graphics, or icons. *Related term:* Visual aids.

Wait time

A pause to give learners time to reflect on questions posed.

Web-based training

Synchronous or asynchronous instruction delivered over the Internet. *Related terms:* Internet- or Intranet-based training; Web-based instruction.

NOTE

1. This glossary was developed by Marguerite Foxon, Ph.D., Principal Performance Technologist at Motorola, Inc. and ibstpi member (1997–2005) with assistance from J. Michael Spector and James D. Klein.

ABOUT THE AUTHORS

James D. Klein, Ph.D., is a Professor in the Educational Technology program at Arizona State University, Tempe. He serves as a member and Treasurer of the International Board of Standards for Training, Performance and Instruction (ibstpi). Previously, he served as development editor of *Educational Technology Research & Development* (ETR&D) and as president of the Design and Development Division (D&D) and the Research and Theory Division of the Association for Educational Communications and Technology. He has been recognized as an outstanding alumnus of the Instructional Systems program at Florida State University and for his service to D&D. Dr. Klein's research, teaching, and consulting activities are in the areas of instructional design, strategies for active learning, and performance improvement.

J. Michael Spector, Ph.D., is Associate Director of the Learning Systems Institute and Professor in the Instructional Systems program at Florida State University. He serves as Executive Vice President of ibstpi and as development editor of *ETR&D*. Previously, he was Professor and Chair of Instructional Design, Development and Evaluation at Syracuse University, Professor of Information Science, and Director of the Educational Information Science and Technology Research Program at the University of Bergen, Norway, and the Senior Scientist for Instructional Systems Research at the United States Air Force Armstrong Research Laboratory. He is a distinguished graduate of the United States Air Force Academy and earned a Ph.D. in Philosophy from the University of Texas at Austin. Dr. Spector's research is in the area of learning and instructional science with special interest in intelligent support for instructional design and assessing learning in complex domains.

Barbara Grabowski, Ph.D., is Professor of Education in the Instructional Systems Program at Pennsylvania State University. She serves as President

Instructor Competencies: Standards for Face-to-Face, Online, and Blended Settings, pages 131–132
Copyright © 2004 by Information Age Publishing
All rights of reproduction in any form reserved.

of ibstpi. Previously, she has been Principal Investigator of two major research and design grants with the U.S. National Aeronautics and Space Administration (NASA). Prior to working at Penn State, she was a designer, developer and evaluator for a distance delivery program for nuclear reactor operators, and designer of multimedia materials for industry, the military, and medical environments. This prior experience drives her main research on pedagogical and administrative issues related to learning with technology and through the World Wide Web. She has been nationally and internationally recognized by the International University Continuing Education Association for the programs she has developed, and received an outstanding book award for *Individual Differences: Learning and Instruction* (with Jonassen).

Ileana de la Teja, Ph.D., is a Researcher at the Cognitive Informatics and Learning Environments Research Centre (LICEF), Télé-université, in Montreal, Canada. She serves as a member and Secretary of ibstpi. She completed her Ph.D. and MA degrees in Instructional Technology at the University of Montreal and has participated in multiple Canadian and international projects. She has worked with professional associations, private and public organizations, and universities in Chile, Italy, Mexico, Norway, and the United States. Dr. de la Teja's interest domains include instructional design methodology for e-learning environments, online learning competencies, learning objects and international standards in learning design, as well as evaluation.

AUTHOR INDEX

Instructor Competencies: Standards for Face-to-Face, Online, and Blended Settings, pages 133–135
Copyright © 2004 by Information Age Publishing
All rights of reproduction in any form reserved.

SUBJECT INDEX

Instructor Competencies: Standards for Face-to-Face, Online, and Blended Settings, pages 137–141
Copyright © 2004 by Information Age Publishing
All rights of reproduction in any form reserved.